W9-BSV-232

ALSO BY JOE LIEBERMAN

The Power Broker

The Scorpion and the Tarantula

The Legacy of Child Support in America

In Praise of Public Life
(with Michael D'Orso)

AN AMAZING ADVENTURE

Joe and Hadassah's Personal Notes on the 2000 Campaign

Joe and Hadassah Lieberman

with Sarah Crichton

Simon & Schuster

New York London Toronto Sydney Singapore

SIMON & SCHUSTER
Rockefeller Center
1230 Avenue of the Americas
New York, NY 10020

For information about special discounts for bulk purchases,
please contact Simon & Schuster Special Sales:
1-800-456-6798 or business@simonandschuster.com

Designed by Jeanette Olender
Manufactured in the United States of America

1 3 5 7 9 10 8 6 4 2

Library of Congress Cataloging-in-Publication Data
Lieberman, Joseph I.
An amazing adventure : Joe and Hadassah's personal notes on the
2000 campaign / Joe and Hadassah Lieberman ; with Sarah Crichton.
p. cm.
1. Presidents—United States—Election—2000. 2. United States—Politics and
government—1993–2001. 3. Lieberman, Joseph I. 4. Lieberman, Hadassah.
5. Vice-Presidential candidates—United States—Biography. 6. Legislators—United
States—Biography. 7. Legislator's spouses—United States—Biography.
8. Political campaigns—United States.
I. Lieberman, Hadassah. II. Crichton, Sarah. III. Title.
E889 .L54 2003
324.973'0929—dc21
2002030677
ISBN 0-7432-2938-X

To the people of Connecticut
for their steadfast support over more than three
decades, without which we would never have had
the opportunity we were given in 2000.

and

To the people of America
for the warmth with which they greeted us
on our amazing adventure.

AN AMAZING ADVENTURE

CHAPTER ONE

It's hard to call friends with bad news, but on that Sunday night, two of my friends did. Jim Kennedy, my former press secretary, who worked with Al Gore in the White House, called to say: "They're going to leak the name to the press in time for the Monday morning news shows." Although he hadn't gotten official notice about Gore's choice of a running mate, Jim said signs were pointing increasingly to Senator John Edwards of North Carolina.

Then Dan Gerstein, my press secretary, called. "I hate to be the one to tell you, Senator, but I've just heard from somebody at one of the networks. It's going to be Edwards."

So that was that. We'd known a decision was imminent; Gore had vowed to announce his selection by Monday. My wife, Hadassah, and our twelve-year-old daughter, Hani, had tried to stay busy to keep distracted, but it wasn't really working. My eighty-five-year-old mother had been so excited and anxious that she'd come up to New Haven from her home in Stamford, Connecticut, saying, "I've just got to be with you. Win or lose, I want to be in the house with you." Our thirty-two-year-old son, Matt, and my younger sister Ellen and her husband, Bert, all of whom live nearby, were over, too. Now I had to let them all know. After gathering the family, I set glasses on the dining room table and opened a bottle of wine.

"Apparently it's not going to happen," I said, adding quickly, "But it's been a great thrill, a great honor, to be considered. We've been very lucky." We had come very close, and in the process, some political barriers had been broken. We toasted one another and America and went to bed thinking it was over.

My alarm went off at 6:55 on Monday morning, August 7, 2000. Sleepily, I clicked on the television. The local anchor was not dispassionate. "Now let me repeat this *very exciting story,*" she said. "The Associated Press is reporting that Vice President Gore has chosen *our very own* Senator Joe Lieberman to be his running mate."

Now I was awake. "Sweetheart, did you hear that?"

Hadassah groaned in her sleep.

"Al chose me," I said. "They just said it on TV."

"Whattt?" Hadassah sat up in bed, stared at the flickering image, then stared back at me in astonishment and said, "Oh, my God, Joey—it's *you*!"

◘ Gore's staff had decided that when the time came to announce the vice presidential running mate, they would break the news through two reporters they trusted. They would give Ron Fournier, the AP's straight-shooting national political reporter, a jump so he could get the story on the wire; then they would call NBC's Claire Shipman so she could be first to have a "package" ready for the 7:00 A.M. news on the *Today* show.

Fournier was told of this general plan early Sunday afternoon, but hour after hour went by, and the call didn't come. Finally it got to be 11:30, and he was still waiting in his office. He called someone at Gore headquarters and asked, "Am I still doing the story? Is it happening tonight?" Yes, he was told, but go home, and we'll call you when we're ready. Fournier went home, sat by the phone, and fell asleep in a living room chair. At 5:45, he was awakened by a call from Chris Lehane, Gore's campaign press secretary.

"We've decided," Lehane said, but there was a catch: "You've got to guess who it is." A little Lehane five-in-the-morning humor.

Fournier later told me what he'd said. "Well, I've been picking up the leaks all weekend, so I'll have to go with John Edwards."

Lehane said no.

"John Kerry."

No.

"I knew it. You're going to the Midwest!" And Fournier named someone who hadn't been mentioned lately, Indiana senator Evan Bayh.

No.

Fournier told me he then suddenly broke out in goose

bumps. "You're going to make history, and I'm going to write it. It's Lieberman."

Lehane said yes.

It's a wonderful story, and it still chokes me up when I tell it because of Fournier's sense of the improbability that there would be a Jewish candidate on a major ticket.

I got out of bed, threw some water on my face, and headed downstairs to make coffee. I passed Hani's room and she called out, "Daddy, who is it?"

"It's me," I said, and she started screaming, hugged me, and then I just kept walking down the stairs. I was basically in my boxers, heading for the coffeemaker, when I looked up. Two TV cameras peered down at me through our kitchen window. I ducked—and ran upstairs to put on some clothes.

As the phone began to ring and everything began to swirl around us, I realized I needed to get hold of myself, so I did what I do every morning: I said my morning prayers, essentially the same prayers that observant Jews have said for centuries in very different places and very different circumstances. I added some special prayers of gratitude and also added pleas for the strength and ability I knew I would need in the days ahead.

We had only recently allowed ourselves the thought that this day might come. In June I'd been told that I'd made it to Gore's "short list" of potential running mates, but I hadn't known for sure who the other contenders were until Gore let his campaign staff leak a list to the press later in July. On it were Senators John Kerry, Bob Graham, Evan Bayh, Tom Harkin, and John Edwards, House minority leader Dick Gephardt, New Hampshire governor Jeanne Shaheen, former Senate majority leader George Mitchell, and former treasury secretary Bob Rubin. And there was me. We were all part of what Hadassah called "the bouncing boxes," the disembodied heads you'd see bounce up as a graphic on your favorite cable news channel.

Earlier in the spring of 2000, when my name first started surfacing as a potential running mate, I told my old friend and political consultant Carter Eskew (who happened to be advising another old friend of his, Al Gore) that while I didn't expect to be chosen as the VP candidate, I sure hoped I would make it to the short list. I had also talked about that with one of my closest friends and counselors, Al From of the Democratic Leadership Council (DLC), early in January 2000.

"Should you aspire to be on the ticket?" Al asked. "It never hurts to be on a national ticket unless you flop. It doesn't even hurt a vice presidential nominee to be on the losing ticket," he added, "as long as there aren't negative revelations about you and you don't look ill prepared to be president during the campaign. It didn't hurt Hubert Humphrey to run for VP, and it didn't hurt Bob Dole or Ed Muskie to run and lose."

6

It wasn't until May that I was "officially" approached to see if I was willing to be considered. It was the Monday after Hani's bat mitzvah in Connecticut. Former secretary of state Warren Christopher was heading up the search for Gore's running mate, and he asked me if I was interested. "As my twelve-year-old daughter would say, it would be awesome," I told him, "literally awesome, because of my respect for the office. I don't expect to be chosen, but I would be honored to be considered."

By June, Christopher had narrowed down the list of thirty or forty possibilities to fewer than ten contenders. When I learned I had made the cut, well, my hopes grew. I still didn't *expect* to be picked, but I sure wanted to be. For almost thirty years, I had devoted my life to public service, and now I was in reach of an extraordinary opportunity. After ten years as a state senator, six years as Connecticut's attorney general, and two terms as a U.S. senator, I felt ready.

As the vetting process went on through June and July, the odds that I would get the nomination seemed to grow slimmer—at least in public speculation. By August, the folks on the Sunday morning talk shows were saying that Edwards had moved into the lead, followed by Kerry. What seemed to be holding me back was that I wasn't part of the traditional Democratic Party apparatus as some of the others were; my independent, centrist philosophy meant that I was not the first choice of some of the important Democratic interest groups. And the fact that I'm an observant Jew was apparently making some people close to the cam-

Joe and Hadassah on the big screen in Los Angeles.

paign uncomfortable. It wasn't my faith per se, it was the fact that no one could predict how voters would take it. Would my religion become a factor in a close race? Was it worth the risk to see if the country was ready for a Jewish vice president?

The Democratic National Convention was coming up fast, and Gore needed to name his running mate, but the decision wasn't coming easily. All day Sunday, August 6, and into the night in his Nashville hotel suite, he weighed the possibilities with the people he trusted most—his brother-in-law Frank Hunger, Warren Christopher, campaign chairman Bill Daley, Tipper, and the rest of the Gore family. Later in the evening, he met with senior political advisers, including Bob Shrum, Carter Eskew, Tad Devine, Mike Whouley, and campaign manager Donna Brazile. Each argued on behalf of his or her favorite candidate, but by the time they left around 9:30 or so, the consultants still had no sense of what the vice president would do.

One of them later told me that they went back to somebody's room at the hotel for a drink and, laughing, decided they were so clueless, they might as well spin a bottle to see if they could predict whom Gore would choose. Shrum represented Edwards, Whouley was Kerry, and Eskew stood in for me. Three times they spun the bottle—and each time it pointed to Eskew. Donna Brazile, who had earlier told Gore she was for me, flipped a quarter twice between me and John Edwards, and both times it came out on my side. The next day she gave the coin—a Connecticut quarter—to our son Matt.

I'm not superstitious; I certainly don't believe I was picked because of a spinned bottle or a flip of the coin. I do think my chances were helped by what Warren Christopher reportedly said to Gore that Sunday. The choice you're about to make, he told Al, says "what's in your heart, what's in your soul, what's in your mind—and you have to make this choice with that consideration. It's more about you than about whom you choose."

In 1992, there had been media speculation that I was being considered for vice president by Bill Clinton, but I knew it couldn't be serious because I wasn't being vetted. You *know* when you're being vetted. As I learned in 2000, it is a remarkable experience—exhaustive and demanding. When Warren Christopher called to tell me I had made it to the short list and that they would soon have to start vetting me, he warned, "Are you still willing to go forward with it, because it's not easy, and it can be a painful process, and there's no way I can reduce the pain." So I said, "Chris [which is how he is known], you mean this is kind of like having a colonoscopy without anesthesia?" Chris laughed and agreed.

By the time you are chosen, the people running the presidential campaign have a very clear sense of who you are. A vetting team of several people (eight in my case) has analyzed the answers to the enormous number of questions you've been asked. They've pored over your financial records and read every word you've ever written—in my case, four books, countless op-ed articles, and even editorials I wrote for the *Yale Daily News* as an undergraduate in the 1960s. They have interviewed not only the woman you are married to, but the woman you used to be married to. Almost the first question they asked Betty Haas, my former wife, was, "Did you have any reason to suspect that he was having extramarital relations?" "Did he ever use drugs?" Thank God, two easy-to-answer questions with nice, clean answers. Betty apparently joked: "Well, I tried to get him to try marijuana, but the square just wouldn't."

The team investigating me was headed by Jamie Gorelick, a well-known Washington attorney, then at Fannie Mae. I had known Jamie a bit, not well, when she was at the Defense Department and the Justice Department in the Clinton administration; she is very impressive. Because being vetted is arduous, time-consuming, and pressured, I decided to retain someone to represent me and guide me through the process. Jonathan Sallet had been my friend since we worked together on the 1992 Democratic platform. He is a very smart and well-connected lawyer who happened to have just left a good corporate job and so was available. As it turned out, Jonathan and Jamie had practiced law together in their early careers, and their working relationship was strong. That was immensely helpful. Even more helpful, though, was that Sallet and I developed a strategy not simply for surviving the vetting, but for pursuing the nomination.

11

You're not supposed to campaign for the vice presidential nomination. You can't even acknowledge that you are under consideration for it. Early in May, at the end of our first meeting, I asked Warren Christopher, "What should I tell the media, if they ask?"

"You can tell them that I came to see you," he said, "but don't tell them anything you said."

When Chris called a month later to say I had made the short list, I asked again, not only because I wanted to play this by their rules, but because I also realized that how I handled the situation was, in and of itself, a test. "This time," he said, "I don't want you to say *anything*." I didn't. Most of my staff didn't know, our friends didn't know.

I had awkward moments with two of my colleagues in the Senate who were said to be on the short list. One, a jokester who I'm not certain was ever on it, said, "Did you get that questionnaire from Warren Christopher? Boy, that was amazing, wasn't it?"

"What questionnaire?" I said. (There was no questionnaire, at least not one that I ever filled out.)

The other guy, who was definitely on the list, said quietly, "What an experience this is! Kind of amazing, isn't it?" I stopped the conversation. I felt bad afterward that I had been abrupt with him, but I was intent on keeping this secret.

The vetting team's mission is to uncover everything negative about you; they look for reasons why the presidential nominee should *not* pick you. But, presumably, there are also arguments that can be made *for* you. What Sallet and I decided was this: We would not only work to reassure the team that there were no skeletons in my closet, we would also figure out ways to present positive reasons to choose me.

We began by describing the similar senatorial records of Al Gore and me. We had both been certifiable New Democrats, early members of the centrist Democratic Leadership Council. We had both served on the Armed Services Committee and had solid experience in foreign and defense policy. We both chose environmental protection, new economy growth, and governmental efficiency as personal priorities. The policy differences between us were rare; therefore our coming together on a ticket would be comfortable.

We also decided we needed to reach out, in a very discreet way, to a very few people who we thought might be talking to Gore about this selection. We also needed to communicate softly with constituencies within the Democratic Party—especially those I wasn't sure would favor me. The trial lawyers were mad at me because of my support for tort reform as a way to protect small businesses and consumers. The teachers unions were concerned about my support for a demonstration voucher scholarship program for poor children that their families could use to send them to nonpublic schools. I'd also had differences with organized labor over my commitment to trade because I believe it creates jobs. I needed them on my side, or at the very least not set against me. I didn't need to be everyone's first choice, but if somebody close to Gore said, "Hey, he's thinking about Joe Lieberman, what do you think?" I needed these groups to say, "We like him." Or, "He may not be our first choice, but he's fine." Or even, "If Gore wants him, we can live with that."

These contacts were to be made subtly, quietly. Some people on their own initiative made the case for me during the vetting process itself, when they appeared before tribunals of lawyers and researchers to answer questions about me and my background. Other friends made contacts with leaders of the key Democratic constituency groups. My Connecticut colleague Senator Chris Dodd was indispensable. I can still see the scene when I asked for his help. It was the first week of July, and Chris and I were in Branford, Connecticut, with Rosa DeLauro, our New Haven congresswoman, to announce federal aid to the lobster industry, which had been suffering terribly because a rare disease had struck the lobster pools. It was a clear, sunny day on Long Island Sound. I took Chris aside and said, "I've got to talk to you."

Even though there was a lot of local media around, we managed to drift away, walking down a dirt road along the harbor shore. "Warren Christopher called. I'm on the short list," I said. "I'm not supposed to talk to anyone about this, but you're my friend and my colleague, and I wanted to tell you and ask for your counsel."

Chris Dodd responded with generosity and good advice. "Joe, this is a moment of opportunity in your life. You have no way of knowing whether anything like this will ever happen again. You should make sure you do everything you can so you will never look back to this time and say, 'If I had done just one more thing, I might have been the vice presidential nominee.' Of course I understand that you can't go out and campaign for it," he added, "but others can help." He offered to make a few calls quietly to some of those groups that I mentioned.

Al Gore met privately with each of the short list contenders. My turn came early one morning in late July, when I was smuggled into the U.S. Naval Observatory, the vice president's official residence, in the backseat of a van with darkened windows. Over breakfast, Gore said that this was awkward because we were friends, but he had to interview me.

I told him not to worry. I knew how important this decision was, and he should feel comfortable asking whatever he wanted to know. He then proceeded to ask, in essence, "Why should I pick you?" I told him that while it felt surreal and immodest to say these words, I thought he could make the case to the voters that, based on my public service experience in the federal and state governments, I was qualified to become president should that ever become necessary. I also said that because our policy priorities were so similar, and because we were both so-called New Democrats, we would blend together comfortably. And I added that because we were friends, he could absolutely trust me. Al went on to ask questions about some specific issues, then said, "Let's talk about some of the groups in the party, and how they might feel if you were picked."

Okay, I said.

Well, how about . . . labor? How do you think they'd react if you were chosen?

I've got some very good friends in labor, and Chris Dodd talked to so-and-so and he says they're going to be all right.

I see, said Gore. And the African American community. How do you think you'll fare there?

Oh, I said, I've got some good personal relationships with people in the Congressional Black Caucus, and Chris says he's had good conversations there, too.

"So, Joe, is Chris Dodd your John the Baptist?"

"In a manner of speaking," I answered.

When you come in as a VP candidate, you're boarding a train that's already moving. In fact, it's been heading in a direction not just for months, but for years before they hook your car up. It's a great journey you are starting on—and it's a wonderfully decorated car—but you're late.

By the time Al Gore called to offer me the spot—which was late that Monday morning in August—my new campaign staff was in the air, flying from his headquarters in Nashville to New Haven to come get me. "I want you to know there's a team already in place; we've put it together for you," Al said. "They're very experienced—and heading in your direction. They should be landing in New Haven any moment now."

Minutes after we hung up, the doorbell rang and I was leading my new campaign team down into the Bunker, which is what we call our basement. There's not much down there—a couch, a computer, a television, a telephone, a fax. The walls are sixteen-inch-thick poured concrete; it's cool and private. The visitors included my new campaign manager, Tom Nides, who was on leave from Fannie Mae, a veteran of previous national campaigns, and a former aide to former Gore campaign chairman Tony Coelho. Tina Flournoy, my new political director, was a lawyer who had worked with the late Ron Brown at the DNC, and was now with the American Federation of Teachers; Paul Orzulak, my new speechwriter, had written for President Clinton and for Sandy Berger at the National Security Council. Kiki Moore McLean, press secretary, had worked with the Gores off and on since 1992 and was a battle-trained professional. I knew Kiki from her days at the DLC, and I liked her, but I had never met any of the others before.

I've run for political office since 1970, have been a U.S. senator since 1988; I already had a terrific and dedicated staff, eager to take off with me. But this team that Gore sent was experienced at running national campaigns. More than that, *this* was the team Nashville wanted. *Nashville* It became more than a place to me. As the campaign went on, when somebody like Kiki or Nides would say, "Nashville would like you to do this," I'd say, "Wait a second—'Nashville'? There aren't many places you can speak of that way: the Vatican, The Hague, maybe 'Houston.' But 'Nashville'? Who in Nashville wants me to do this?"

If John Edwards had been chosen as Gore's running mate, these people would have flown to North Carolina that day. If Al had picked John Kerry, they would have been in Boston. But they were in my home, sketching out the week's whirlwind schedule.

- Fly to Tenn. this aft. Dinner with Gores. Staff mtg. at hotel after dinner to discuss plans and Dem. Convention, next week.
- Tomorrow, announcement speeches at War Memorial in Nashville.
- Wed., fly to hometowns of VP and Sen. (Carthage, TN, Stamford, CT.)
- Thursday, VP and Sen. to Atlanta for rally with five Southern Dem. governors; Hadassah and Tipper to H's hometown of Gardner, MA.

In a matter of hours, I would go from being the junior senator of a relatively small (though clearly wonderful) state, to being the first Jewish American candidate for national office in American history. If all eyes weren't yet upon us, most soon would be. "Miracles happen!" That's what I told reporters waiting outside my house that first morning. Hadassah quickly came up with her own description—"Magical trauma!"

Upstairs, Philip Dufour was in our bedroom, working his way through Hadassah's closet. *Did she have something to wear when she walked off the plane in Nashville? Something to wear to the rally tomorrow? A nice pantsuit, perhaps?* Dufour was Tipper Gore's great gift to Hadassah. To all of us. Al had said, "I know how tough the transition can be; I've been through it. I want to do everything I possibly can to make it easy for you, and Tipper will do the same for Hadassah." Philip was manager of the vice president's residence, personable and superbly efficient. Here's Hadassah's description of that memorable scene:

◈ Philip knew what we needed to know. What clothes we'd need, how much to pack. Plus, he worked beautifully with Edie. Edie Goldberg is one of my oldest friends. The minute she heard the news about Joe, she came running over. "How much luggage do you have—and how does it look?" she said as she walked through the door. Edie's a take-charge kind of person, which has been a blessing for us before. Eighteen years ago, she'd taken charge of our lives. She had known Joe from his synagogue in New Haven. Down in Riverdale, New York, I was in the process of getting divorced (as was Joe), and Edie decided we would make a good match—even though Joe was a politician and she doesn't usually trust politicians. "But this one," she told me, "looks you in the eye. I think you'll like him." She was right.

So here you had this Orthodox Jewish woman from Connecticut and this French Catholic guy from Louisiana, and you should have heard them going through my things: What length were my skirts? How were my shoes? (Too scuffed.) Panty hose without runs? What color? And it wasn't just me we had to worry about. What about the kids? And what about our new candidate here?

The first logistical challenge was to figure out how to usher an assortment of delirious Liebermans through a swarm of press and neighbors into a waiting motorcade, which, escorted by motorcycle cops with sirens sounding, would take us to Tweed New Haven Airport to board our chartered jet to Nashville. There was Hani and my mother, Marcia; Matt; his wife, April. Our daughter Rebecca, age thirty-one, was on Cape Cod and would fly down later in the day, as would Ethan Tucker, our twenty-five-year-old, and his wife, Ariela Migdal. En route from Seattle, Ethan and Ariela were waiting at Dulles Airport in Washington, D.C., to hear if they were vacation-bound for North Carolina or Nashville-bound for the campaign! My longtime state political director Sherry Brown was there, too, for the flight to Nashville.

Dave O'Brien, our new trip director sent from Nashville, took over. Dave is one of those political operatives who appears quadrennially to work on national campaigns. He's from Massachusetts and started out in 1988 with Mike Dukakis. Then he was involved with the 1992 and 1996 Clinton-Gore campaigns, with, of course, normal jobs in between. "Here's how we're going to do it," Dave said. The children walk out to their cars first, followed by my mother. Then, after a pause, Hadassah and me.

I called everybody together in a circle in the center of our kitchen for a prayer. I thanked God, I thanked my family, I thanked everyone for their help and encouragement. And I said I was going to need them all and God's help in the weeks ahead.

While Dave focused on the nitty-gritty, Kiki McLean kept sight of the big picture. As we were getting ready to walk out of the house in New Haven, she leaned over and whispered, "Sir"—she always called me "sir"—"Sir, don't stop to talk to the press or anybody else on the way out. Just get in the car." I have great respect and affection for Kiki, but she and I jousted throughout the campaign, and this was the first of many small struggles over how to deal with the press. It has been my career-long habit to stay accessible to the media, and by and large, I've been treated fairly by them. But Kiki's seasoned approach was different; she thought it was important to *manage* relations with the press. And one way to do that was to manage access so as not to step on your story if it's a good story.

◈ Little did I know the campaign had really begun. Suddenly you feel you've been body-snatched. You're in a bubble—no, a capsule. You're on a mission. You've got a timetable, and nothing is going to slow you down. You're not allowed to stop and put your arms around your neighbors and friends. They cannot get close enough to hug or touch you. Even exiting the house becomes a rapidly executed orchestration.

When we leave the house, we always kiss the mezuzah, the small wooden box with Torah portions in it that's nailed to the door frame. That's a routine gesture for us, but this time, I almost forget to kiss it until Joey reminds me to. There I am, in prime time, as the press films me doing something I do every time I leave the house.

Yes, my husband has been in public life. Yes, he's a senator. But this is different.

◘ As we walked out, I looked over at the reporters staked out in the forsythia bushes next to my driveway. "Senator Lieberman, over here! Joe, come on over!" I saw Mark Davis, who'd been on Channel 8, the ABC affiliate in New Haven, forever. He'd covered me since I ran for the Senate in 1988, and he was a radio talk show host. And there was Tom Monahan from Channel 30 in Hartford, whom I had known since I was in the state senate in the early seventies. I thought, How can I not go over and talk to Mark and

Tom? So I walked over. I didn't say much, but I couldn't just pass them by.

Kiki leaned in. "Sir," she said, "the first reactions to your selection are well beyond anything any of us had hoped for. *Don't talk. Just get in the car.*"

Our amazing adventure had begun.

CHAPTER TWO

◈ You are always being watched. This is not paranoia, this is just the new reality. So the thing is, how do you maintain any semblance of normalcy? Do you just give up and not try?

There's garbage to be taken out. We're leaving New Haven soon for Nashville, so I have to carry it out to the garage. I don't have any shoes on. We've just learned my husband is running for the second highest office in the land. I'm trying to figure it all out, and suddenly there are all these media people falling out of the forsythia bushes, aiming cameras at my face. They're saying, "What are you doing? How are you doing?" The next thing you know, people around the country are watching me take out the trash: barefoot!

◘ We weren't naive. We knew that if I was selected, our lives would become open books. When it had begun to look as if I might be a serious contender, Mike Berman, who'd been Vice President Fritz Mondale's chief of staff, sent an unsettling but essential piece of advice our way. "Tell Joe," he told my chief of staff, Bill Andresen, "to go home and sit at the table across from Hadassah, and have them both look each other in the eye, and then say to each other: 'Is there anything you haven't told me about your life? Because if this goes forward, whatever it is, it's going to come out.'"

Not only was I aware of this part of contemporary American political life, I had made it clear I believe a politician should be reconciled to it. On September 4, 1998, I publicly criticized my old friend Bill Clinton for his relationship with Monica Lewinsky. In a twenty-four-minute speech delivered from the floor of the Senate, I argued that "the inescapable truth is that the president's private conduct can and often does have profound public consequences." Because of this fact, I said, "Whether he or we think it fair or not, the reality . . . is that a president's private life is public."

I had become furious at the president's inadequate assumption of responsibility during his grand jury testimony a few weeks earlier, and the more I thought about it, the more I concluded I had a responsibility to say so publicly. It was time for a Democrat and a supporter of the president's to call him to task. There must be "some measure of public rebuke" for President Clinton, I said. His behavior was not only "disgraceful," but "immoral" and "harmful, for it sends a message of what is acceptable behavior to the larger American family—particularly to our children—which is as influential as the negative messages communicated by the entertainment culture." It is "embarrassing . . . not just for him and his family," I said, "it is embarrassing for all of us as Americans."

◈ In the weeks before Joe made the Lewinsky speech, as the pressure built up and up in D.C., we'd arranged for a short escape to a beautiful beach in Madison, Connecticut, where, I had fantasized, we could just walk and talk and eat with our children. No such luck. We couldn't go anywhere the summer of 1998 without someone stopping Joe to tell him about their disappointment, or anger, or support of the president. Then they'd ask Joe how he could attack Hollywood for its immorality and irresponsibility and stay silent about the president's behavior. Even our family dinners became debates—with our children angry at Clinton and his mother defending the president.

It became clear he had to speak out; he couldn't stay silent on this. Joe has always been an independent thinker and a straight shooter. There have been times when he's annoyed fellow Democrats because he puts his personal values before party interests. He's been tough on the entertainment industry, and that's rattled some Democrats. But both of us have felt as parents that it's been an important thing for Joe to do. And he's never been afraid to reach across the aisle if he thinks he's found a like-minded lawmaker. When the Senate has been polarized, Republicans against Democrats, Joe often refuses to go automatically along party lines.

But to stand on the floor of the Senate and be the first Democratic senator to come forward and condemn the behavior of the president, I have to think that was the most difficult, wrenching day of Joe's political career.

We were sitting in our kitchen in Washington, D.C., the night before he was going to give the speech on the Senate floor. I knew what he was going to say, but I was afraid. "Joe, don't do this," I said. "You can't criticize the president in public. How do you know how this will affect your political career?"

He looked at me in disbelief. The joke between us has always been my persistent question—"How long before you can go private and make some money?"

"Since when do you care about my political career?" Joe said. "I've made the decision. I've got to do this. I can't turn back."

So when the press in 2000 analyzed what Joe brought to the ticket, I wasn't surprised when they emphasized his determination to say what he believed. I had personally witnessed this.

I always wondered what feelings my friend Bill Clinton carried around within him about me after my speech, but he could not have been more gracious or more enthusiastic when he called to congratulate me that Monday in August when I was selected. He even had some advice about how to handle my speech about him. "Now, Joe," he said, "you know the press may bring up your speech." I agreed that was likely. He said, "Well, you just tell them, 'I stand by what I said in that speech. And President Clinton himself has said he agreed with me.' Tell them we've known each other thirty years, and of course you were disappointed in my behavior. But you can also remind them that you fought against impeachment because you knew that whatever people felt about me personally, two-thirds of them thought I was doing a good job as president and that I didn't deserve to be impeached. And I know you agreed with them, Joe, and I remember you argued that the framers of the Constitution could not have intended for impeachment to be used in a case like this. In fact, the impeachment was an abuse of power that should make the voters reluctant to give control of the Presidency and Congress to the Republicans this fall. Then, if they ask you about it again during the campaign, you can tell them you already answered those questions." (Interestingly, I wouldn't be asked much about it all during the campaign.)

Bill Clinton and I met when he was at Yale Law School and volunteered for my first political campaign in 1970. He went door-to-door to get me elected to the Connecticut State Senate, and we've been friends ever since. We've shared much of the same political philosophy and emerged from the same New Democratic political movement. Clinton is a brilliant policy formulator and political strategist. He cares about people, conveys that caring as well as anyone I have known, and has a progressive, layered, and very real sense of America and the American people.

Right from the start of Campaign 2000 in that first phone conversation, he offered me valuable advice. He remembered a speech I had given at the National Prayer Breakfast earlier that year on the appropriate role for faith in our public life; he urged me to circulate it widely. Stand strong against those who might question your religious beliefs and behavior, he said. There will be some people in the campaign who will try to keep you quiet on this, but don't you hesitate to talk about your religion. And when it comes to your refusal to campaign on the Sabbath, he said, "some people are going to start saying to you, 'Gee, how can you give up one of the optimum campaign days on Saturday by not campaigning?' If they say that, just tell them to go straight to hell!" I laughed heartily at that.

Clinton had a clear recommendation about how his vice president should handle the record of the preceding eight years. "Al should get credit for what the administration did right but not get blamed for my mistakes, which were personal and not public. The American people are too fair and too smart to vote against him for that. By choosing you as his running mate, Al has freed himself from being defensive about my personal mistakes. He can now go out and talk about all that we've done for the country over the last eight years. I know you're proud of our record, Joe, so it will be easy for you to talk about how you will build on the prosperity and progress."

Finally, he offered me good advice on how I should describe the Republican ticket: "Our opponents are not bad people. They love their families and their country. But we have honest disagreements with them. Ideas have consequences. And they have some bad ideas.

"You know all that, Joe," he said. "Just be what you are."

◈ On the plane to Nashville, people begin to treat Joey differently.

"Senator, would you like a pillow?"

"Senator, would you like a snack?"

"Senator, would you like some tea?"

"Senator, can I squeeze your teabag?"

He's going to have to watch out, I think, or his head's going to get swollen from all this attention. And I have to learn to tune this out in the time we travel together.

◘ When we land, a phalanx of press is waiting, but they've been lined up at a distance. For the first time, but as would happen every day for the rest of the campaign, Dave O'Brien and Kiki McLean have everyone exit the plane before us. Then they get off, too, but Dave returns to say,

"There are cameras at nine o'clock," or twelve o'clock, or *wherever* the cameras are. "As you come out of the plane, pause, and wave to the cameras."

That first day, landing in Nashville, before we exit the narrow plane door, I lean in to Hadassah and say, "Sweetie, do me a favor. Just take one step down and I'll stand on the top step." I was thinking of the narrow door and the cameras Dave had just told us were out there.

◈ I think, Oh my God. What is he doing? Choreographing our exit from the plane?

▣ Yes, sweetheart, so we wouldn't be squeezed in that narrow door for the picture. Incidentally, it *was* a lovely picture: Hadassah and me waving from the top of the steps. And it ran all over America.

◈ I decided that it was critical for me to remain normal, but I often had to convince staff that it was okay to show the public my vulnerabilities—in a national way.

The first time she meets me, my campaign manager, Sally Aman, points straight at my shoes, basic two-year-old black pumps on sale at Nordstrom, and says,

"What are those?" And I say, "What?" And she says, "Oh, no . . . no, those . . . no, you can't . . . those are just *unacceptable.*"

On the one hand, I understand the importance of looking nice, and I like to look nice; I like nice clothes, nice hair. I understand why everyone keeps worrying about what I'm going to wear; I'm going to be on constant public view. But at a certain level, it starts getting pretty crazy. You think one afternoon with Philip Dufour and Edie Goldberg took care of the clothes issue? Forget it. "We're going to have to totally re-dress you, poor thing," says Sally, and less than a week after Joe's been picked, four giant boxes of clothes, containing roughly thirty outfits each, arrive at our town house in Georgetown. That's 120 outfits for me to try on, friends! We hang the clothes on racks that collapse under the weight, nearly crushing poor Melissa Winter, Joe's executive assistant, who is here to help (and ends up buying a few of the outfits herself).

Total strangers are rummaging through the stacks and rating me as I run up and down the stairs to try them on and model them all. "No, yes, no, yes." Who are these people? No to the stripes; it won't be photogenic. Yes to the purple pantsuit with the pink lining! (TV loves strong colors.) In the end, I choose half a dozen new outfits, and my brother, Ary Freilich, bless him, winds up paying for them as a gift.

I'm trying to be a good sport, but there's a part of me that gets my back up when I feel that people are pushing me around. I feel rebellious, like a teenager. My independence is important to me. Part of me just wants to say, "Hey, slow down, cool it! You don't like these shoes? Well, I'm wearing them whether you like it or not!" So many times I wanted to say, "Who really cares about my hair?" But reality beckons, and you realize that bad hair days are a luxury not afforded the campaign spouse. You are always on display. You have a role. You need to look "together."

"You say I need some 'campaign-friendly pumps' with two-and-a-half-inch heels? Fine, let's go buy some."

I have come to respect many things about Laura Bush, but one thing in particular speaks volumes to me, although it may sound inconsequential. I read an article that described Laura Bush as carrying her own purse. Do you know what a challenge that is? The "handlers" do not want you dragging your purse around. They say it looks bad and gets in the way. They especially don't like the way it looks when you climb out of a car with one. I had a staff member whose responsibility it was to grab mine. Laura Bush must have just said, I'm carrying my purse, and that was that. Believe me, I was impressed.

◘ We meet our Secret Service agents in Nashville on Tuesday, August 8. Hadassah and I each are assigned two details of agents, which rotated on and off every three weeks. Mike Davis, Manny Velasquez, Betty McDonald, and Dave

Zimmerman led my details; Tom McCarthy, Andy Orringer, Ron Weiss, and Eileen Barry led Hadassah's. On this day they are strangers, but over the next few months we come not only to appreciate their protection, but to respect them all. They are fine professionals, and we ultimately consider them extended family.

Early on, one of them said to us, "Remember this. Remember it all because you're about to have a unique life experience. It's so important that you remember every single part."

◈ **The Secret Service quickly taught us new rules, most of which I'm not going to divulge. But here's one: We could no longer lock any doors to our house or to hotel rooms. They needed to be able to burst in at any moment. The first night we were supposed to sleep in an unlocked hotel bedroom, I had a hard time falling asleep wondering whether the door would fly open.**

Here's another rule: When you're in a car and it pulls up at your destination, your first instinct is to throw open your door—but you *don't*. This is one of the times of maximum vulnerability, so you must always wait until the Secret Service has secured the location, then wait for an agent to open your door. Then, when the door swings open and you climb out? Smile, smile, *smile*. The Secret Service didn't teach us that last part. Our press staff did.

CHAPTER THREE

GORE PICKS LIEBERMAN; RUNNING MATE
TO BE FIRST JEW ON MAJOR TICKET

—*Washington Post*

GORE PICKS LIEBERMAN, A JEW, AS
RUNNING MATE

—*Boston Globe*

GORE SELECTS ORTHODOX JEW AS
RUNNING MATE

—*Chicago Sun-Times*

LIEBERMAN WILL RUN WITH GORE; FIRST
JEW ON A MAJOR U.S. TICKET

—*New York Times*

The morning after my selection was announced, the choice was being hailed as "bold," "daring," "courageous." President Clinton called it "a gutsy move" on Gore's part. The Democratic organization braced for a backlash. As Bill

Daley, the campaign chairman, said, "There was a sense that 'This is a risk; who knows how it will be received?' . . . [H]aving a Jewish candidate was uncharted waters." Even as a Jewish candidate, in some ways, I wasn't a particularly "safe choice." "It's the unspoken rule of American firsts," wrote Michael Powell in *The Washington Post,* that those who break through barriers should be easy-to-swallow choices with "no rough edges." By contrast, as one commentator said of me, "Not only is he Jewish, he's seriously Jewish."

"His speeches are drenched with biblical references and bold prophecies," wrote another reporter.

Drenched with biblical references and bold prophecies? Is that me they're talking about?

The vice president made the formal announcement of my selection at a joyous rally in Nashville on Tuesday, August 8, under a brutally hot sun, a sun so hot that people fainted. I had such a powerful sense of gratitude that day, I felt spontaneously moved at the beginning of my remarks to offer a prayer of gratitude.

"Dear friends," I said, "I am so full of gratitude at this moment. I ask you to allow me to let the spirit move me, as it does, to remember the words from Chronicles, which are 'to give thanks to God'—to give thanks to God and declare His name and make His acts known to the people. To be glad of spirit; to sing to God and make music to God; and most of all, to give glory and gratitude to God, from whom all blessings truly do flow."

The crowd, a national crowd but mostly a Tennessee crowd, echoed amens.

But as I said in a speech to the Democratic Leadership Council a year later, some of the initial "hosannas" rapidly turned to "How dare he's." Concerns began to emerge in the press with my public declarations of faith, and some Democrats seemed very uncomfortable not with my religion, but with my religiosity. Reporters counted the number of times I invoked the name of God in my speeches. The Anti-Defamation League (ADL) called on me to ease up on "overt expressions of religious values and beliefs." A few Democrats respectfully asked me to keep my prayers quiet.

But I didn't, because I wanted to be who I am, and prayer and faith are at the center of my life and of my family's life. The same is true of many Americans, and I have never understood why some people feel that when you go into public life you lose the freedom to talk about your faith. My religious beliefs shape who I am and explain why I have dedicated myself to a life of public service.

At the National Prayer Breakfast earlier in 2000, in the speech President Clinton had urged me to circulate, I had quoted the Catholic theologian Michael Novak: "Americans are starved for good conversations about important matters of the human spirit. In Victorian England, religious devotion was not a forbidden topic of conversation, sex was. In America today, the inhibitions are reversed." Michael is right, and that is why I resolved to keep enjoying my First Amendment rights to both free speech and the free exercise of religion throughout the campaign.

In recent years, I think we've seen clear signs of a new American spiritual awakening. This one began in the hearts of millions of Americans who felt threatened by the vulgarity and violence in our society and turned to religion as the way to rebuild a wall of principle and purpose around themselves and their families. There is compelling evidence that our culture has coarsened, that our sense of right and wrong in the private sector and the public sector has blurred, that our standards of decency and civility have eroded, and that the traditional sources of values in our society—faith, family, and community—are in a struggle with the darker forces of immorality, inhumanity, and greed. And I think this is something that people across the country, of all backgrounds and beliefs, including the nonreligious, share as a concern. I very much wanted to use the opportunity my national candidacy provided to express that shared concern.

We face some real moral challenges today. From the beginning of our existence, Americans have known where to turn in times of moral challenge. John Adams wrote, "Our Constitution was made only for a moral and religious people." Adams understood that in a society where a government has limited powers, and people are free, you need other sources of good behavior, and for many there is none better than faith in God, none better than the belief that every person is created by the same God, and therefore we are all brothers and sisters, and each deserving of equal treatment. That is why we pledge our allegiance, after all, to one nation, under God, and why faith has played such a central role in our nation's history.

The fundamental affirmation of monotheistic faith in Judaism is "Hear, O Israel, the Lord is our God. The Lord is one. Thou shalt love the Lord thy God with all thy heart and all thy soul and all thy might. . . . Thou shalt place these words on the doorposts of your houses and upon your gates." The words of that commandment are found in the Book of Deuteronomy and are spoken by Jesus in the Gospel of Mark, when he is asked to describe the essence of his faith. They are also contained, still today, in the mezuzahs many Jews attach to their doorways. Since childhood, I have followed the custom of kissing the mezuzah on the way in and the way out of my house, as an unspoken plea for God's blessing on my goings and comings. When I reminded Hadassah to kiss the mezuzah as we headed off to Nashville, I was essentially asking her to join me in an act of faith as we began this new chapter of our lives.

While the folks at the Anti-Defamation League and Americans United for the Separation of Church and State nearly had a constitutional coronary over what I was saying and doing, I was convinced that most Americans, including those who are not religious, accepted and respected our religious observance and our willingness to talk about its importance to us. The night before the announcement rally at the War Memorial, during our dinner with the Gores, Al explained how he had handled the question of my religion. "I came to believe," he said, "there was a difference between anti-Semitism and the fear of anti-Semitism. A lot of people told me that your religion would be a problem, but I concluded that their fear of anti-Semitism exceeded anti-Semitism itself. None of these people were themselves anti-Semitic, some were Jewish. But they had an exaggerated sense of how much other people would object to a Jewish candidate. Once I realized that their fear was greater than the reality, I understood that I was free to choose whoever I wanted as my vice presidential candidate without reference to religion."

That took me back to an earlier, interesting conversation. In 1992 , when Bill Clinton was deciding who his running mate would be, I found myself in the senators' rest room adjacent to the Senate chamber. Usually there's an attendant in there, but on this day there were just Al Gore and me. The media were reporting that Gore was on Clinton's short list, so I said to Al what I truly felt: "I've been reading about the vice presidential speculation and I hope you get it, I think you'd be fantastic."

"Thanks," Gore said, "and, you know, we're friends, so I want to tell you an interesting story. Warren Christopher came and talked to me as part of the vetting process, and at the end, he said, 'Is there anyone else you would recommend that we think about?' I want you to know that I mentioned your name."

Needless to say, I was surprised and pleased—then Al added something very interesting. He said, "You know, Chris asked me, 'Do you think voters in Tennessee would support an Orthodox Jew for vice president?' And I told him I didn't think it would be a problem, because Tennesseeans are very religious. They're mostly Baptists, and they will identify with someone who is religiously observant. Besides," he added, "the Old Testament is real to the people in Tennessee, so I think there will be a connection, because Joe lives through the Old Testament and so do they."

"You know and I know that I feel right at home here today because we're all children of the same God." That's what I told the several hundred worshipers of the Reverend Wendell Anthony's Fellowship Chapel in Detroit on August 28. It was my first solo outing after the convention, and I was in the mood to rejoice.

And, for the first time, I had flown on my own campaign plane, a DC-9 with the Gore-Lieberman logo painted in red, white, and blue on its side. We called it the *Spirit,* because it had been leased from Spirit Airlines (which, unbelievably—and unknown to Nashville—was owned by a group of Orthodox Jews from Maryland). That name enabled me to tell the congregants at the predominantly African American church in Detroit that morning that the *Spirit* had moved me there and that I felt the country "moving to a new spiritual awakening." I called for religion to play a greater role in public life. The congregants were with me, shouting *amens*, and they were in agreement too when I urged, "Let's break through some of the inhibitions that have existed to talk together across the flimsy lines of separation of faith, to talk together, to study together, to pray together, and ultimately to sing His holy name together."

And that's exactly what the people at Fellowship Chapel and I did that morning. It was a thrilling, inspiring experience. Unfortunately, not all of my staff was as receptive as the folks in the church. Tom Nides was waiting for me behind the pulpit. He was ashen faced. "What are you doing?" he asked. "Are you *crazy*?"

"You think I got carried away?" I asked Tom, who looked as if his head were about to explode. Most of what I said that morning I had been saying for years in churches, synagogues, and on the senate floor. I thought Tom was overreacting.

"Senator, it was a rock-and-roll show, I'm telling you," Tom recalled later. "I was freaking out, and you just laughed and kept smiling this happy grin."

◈ What people know, when they meet Joe, is that when he says, "God bless you," he means, deeply means, "May God take care of you." People take comfort in that. They take comfort when they are given it, and we take comfort when the prayer is returned to us. People of faith, people who believe deeply in God, understand

that there is something that you share. And I think a lot of people of all faiths feel that about Joe.

It was comforting to me to see Joe praying in our house in New Haven that morning he was chosen. I knew then that this campaign, this possibility, would not change him or change his behavior. His faith gives him a strength and a stability through everything that happens.

The reaction to our religious observances did take some unusual turns. I turned on the TV one night early in the campaign and found Reverend Bob Jones on *Larry King Live,* saying how great it was that I was a person of faith and was willing to talk about it in public. Jerry Falwell and Pat Robertson said similarly positive things, and a few days after my selection was announced, my Republican colleague from Kansas, Sam Brownback, wrote a very nice op-ed piece for *The New York Times* about the importance of my selection because of my faith and willingness to talk about it.

On the other hand, the B'nai B'rith Anti-Defamation League and individual Jews continued to express anxiety about my public religiosity. Clearly, some of that came from Jewish history and memories of state-sponsored anti-Semitism that, to me, had little or no relevance to America today. About a week before I was named, I was in New Haven at an event for my Senate campaign, and a woman I've known forever—a lovely woman, lovely looking, lovely in spirit, probably close to eighty years old—came up to me and said, "I just want to say that I hope Gore *doesn't* ask you to run. And if he does, I plead with you not to accept." It wasn't my personal safety she was worried about. It was what my nomination might do to the safety of the Jewish community. "You know," she said, "if you get elected and the economy goes down, they'll blame us."

I didn't know what to say. Fear of that kind of anti-Semitism is so distant from my experience. Of course, I understand the history behind that woman's anxieties, and I know there are still people who experience anti-Semitism in America today, but it seemed so far from the America I know and love. I grew up in Stamford, Connecticut, which was then a small New England city, very diverse and very tolerant. I never experienced any anti-Semitism. Most of my friends were not Jewish. Yes, they elected me as their class president, but they also walked with me to the class after-prom party because it was on a Friday night and I could not ride in a car on the Sabbath unless it was an emergency.

Hadassah grew up in a similar, tolerant small New England city, Gardner, Massachusetts, where her father was a rabbi and became the head of the Interfaith Ministerial Alliance. In her case, Gardner High School changed the prom to a Saturday night so she could go. Hadassah is the child of Holocaust survivors. Anybody who is Jewish, and most who are not, have been affected by the Holocaust. But not at the level of Holocaust survivors or their children.

Hadassah's mother, Ella Wieder, was a Hungarian Jew who survived Dachau and Auschwitz. Her father, Samuel Freilich, was a lawyer and a rabbi in Prague who could have escaped—he managed to obtain a visa to Australia. But he decided to throw in his lot with his people, and as a result he wound up in a slave labor battalion. Hadassah's parents met and married in Prague after the war, and she was born there in 1948. The three of them came to this country in 1949 when the Communists took over the former Czechoslovakia and my father-in-law concluded that while they had survived the Nazis, by the grace of God, he was not going to risk life under the Communists. So this dark side of Jewish history is very vivid for Hadassah. And she keeps it alive for me, too.

After I was elected to the Senate in November 1988, we flew to Washington about two weeks later for an orientation for the new senators. There were ten of us, five new Democrats and five new Republicans. At one point we were all taken out on the Senate floor and the historian of the Senate spoke about the extraordinary history of the chamber.

When he was finished, we were left to absorb it. Hadassah and I just sat quietly for some time, until she asked, "What are you thinking about, Joey?"

I looked around the great room, and I said, "I have this

sense of wonderment that I'm here. So many of my heroes in public life were here: Teddy Roosevelt (as vice president), Harry Truman, and of course JFK. What are *you* thinking, sweetheart?"

◈ **I said to Joe that I was thinking about how my presence here was a victory, a victory over evil, over people who wanted us dead. Here I am, the daughter of survivors, married to a United States senator in a great free country. And I said, "I'm thinking about how my *fist* is up in the air to Hitler."**

⧈ One of the very first calls of congratulation I received on the morning I was chosen came from the Reverend Jesse Jackson. I told this story repeatedly during the campaign, and I'll keep telling it over and over, too, because it moved me so much and encapsulates my vision of America. I've known Jesse for many years, all the years I've been in the Senate. We've disagreed on one or another issue, but I have great admiration for him and consider him a valued friend. That morning in August, 2000, he called with real enthusiasm and warm congratulations. And he explained why. "In America, when a barrier is broken for one group —or even for just one person—the doors of opportunity open wider for every other American."

What a wonderful expression of the American ideal! Because what he was feeling and saying wasn't just about me, it was about the American promise of opportunity for everyone. And he said it at a time on a day when it wasn't yet clear how America would react to a Jewish candidate for national office. In the end, not only would people react positively and fairly, but my candidacy would be seen precisely the way Reverend Jackson defined it: as delivering the message that we all rise together, that a victory for one is a victory for all, that American democracy is not a zero sum game. For me, the most moving moments of the campaign were when I saw how people who were quite different from me—racially, religiously, ethnically—got excited and empowered by my candidacy.

In Nashville, at the announcement rally, a friend of mine got jostled by a man who was anxiously trying to make his way to the front of the crowd. "Relax," my friend griped. "What are you doing?"

"I'm so sorry," the man said. "I apologize. I just wanted to be the first Arab American to congratulate Senator Lieberman."

In Los Angeles, at a rally of Latino-Americans, a woman held up a sign that summed it all up in two wonderful words, perhaps never before joined together: "Viva Chutzpah."

These reactions probably meant so much to me because the most formative experiences of my political life were in the civil rights movement of the 1960s. In the 2000 campaign, I felt as if I were back in the movement. In African

American churches, in Latino neighborhoods, in gatherings of Native Americans or new Americans or gay and lesbian Americans, all across America I felt not just support for the programs our ticket was advocating, but a powerful sense of shared values and commonly held hopes and dreams, that the barrier broken by my candidacy was a door opening for every other American.

◈ **There were times for us during the campaign when going to the synagogue for a routine Sabbath service took an enormous effort, because people would go crazy. "Oh, my God! You're the hero of the age!" They'd rush out of synagogues to greet us. "It's a breakthrough," they'd say. "It's a *kiddush Hashem*!" Translated, the Hebrew term *kiddush Hashem* means the sanctification of God's name through your actions. It is a weighty compliment, not to be taken lightly.**

At one synagogue, this incredible thing happened. A boy who must have been nine or ten came over to Joe and asked, "Do you mind if I bless you?" And the boy just put his hand on Joe's head and blessed him.

It wasn't just religious Jews who were giving us their blessings. Those feelings spread into so many different groups. People of all religions and races would come to us and say, "We're praying for you, God bless you." Maybe it sounds corny, but the intimacy we had with people, in the midst of my exhaustion, in the midst of

the craziness, gave us strength. It would say to me, "It's okay, sweetheart, it's okay. We're with you."

I have a thousand different memories, of so many people, from so many backgrounds—all reaching out to embrace us, all feeling that they were being represented by us, which is just the way we felt.

Not too long ago, I watched the wonderful television program *The West Wing*. It was a replay of an episode in which the president nominates the first Hispanic to be a Supreme Court justice. I took myself by surprise when I started to tear up at the end because I was so moved by the breakthrough, by the barrier falling—and at the same time it made me think, God, if I hadn't been myself, if I were just some guy out there watching Joe Lieberman get nominated, I would have been bawling. And from what people have told me, I wouldn't have been alone.

As the campaign went on, I had the opportunity to talk to a larger audience than ever before about my values and also about America's values. I had a favorite thought, and it was this: We Americans are a unique people who, from the beginning, did not define our nation according to its borders. We defined America according to our national values and ideals, and the most important of those were freedom and opportunity and responsibility.

Most people have an internal picture of themselves—who they are, what they believe, what their strengths and weaknesses are. It may or may not be an accurate picture, but over time we embrace and accept it.

At some point along the campaign trail, not in a singular moment or place, but in an evolutionary way, Hadassah and I began to understand that others were seeing us differently from how we were seeing ourselves. We had not changed. We were still aware of our limits and flaws. But we had nonetheless become vessels of hope for many people, symbols of their own uniquely American dreams. In that sense, we came to represent some things larger and better than ourselves—the most important of which was the promise of opportunity and community that America makes to each of her children.

CHAPTER FOUR

At the end of day two, Hadassah and I appeared on *Larry King Live* from a beautiful, dark-wood room at Vanderbilt University in Nashville. I was doing fine, laying out my position on everything from the Middle East to the national missile defense system, from late-term abortion to the V-chip, when, reasonably enough, Larry asked me what day I would be delivering my acceptance speech before the Democratic National Convention the next week. I didn't know. I looked over at Hadassah, and she looked as confused as I did. I knew we'd been told, but I guess there's only so much a person can absorb. "I've got to tell you," I said, "yesterday morning seems like about three years ago, Larry."

The night before, we'd celebrated with the Gores. Dinner was in a suite at the Loews Vanderbilt Plaza Hotel. My mother was the first person through the door. She is very sentimental and very patriotic. When I was growing up, she always asked us to sing "God Bless America" at the end of every Passover seder. But Mom is also a strong and proud woman. Leaning on her cane as she came through the door that evening, she looked up, fixed Al in the eye, and said, "Mr. Vice President, you certainly made a *great* choice of running mate!" Both Gores burst out laughing.

Over a glass of wine before dinner, they asked what else they could do to make the transition go smoothly for us. Tipper had assigned her staff the responsibility of telling us how they might help. They were prepared to offer suggestions ranging from how many new phone lines we were going to need in our home to how to handle Hani's trips to the orthodontist in Hadassah's absence. And in addition to loaning us Philip Dufour, Tipper had handpicked Sally Aman, who was her former communications director, to be Hadassah's campaign manager.

It was reassuring to see the extent to which the Gores wanted to help us onto the national stage. Of course, we were old friends, going back to when I first came to the Senate. In 1989, on the first Sabbath of my senatorial career when I had to stay at the Capitol because there was a vote of major importance, Al came over and asked me what I was going to do, where I was going to stay. Oh, don't worry about me, I said. I'm going to sleep on a cot and wash up at the Senate gym.

"Don't do that," said Al. "My folks have an apartment right across the street." He took me over to the perfectly named Methodist Apartments, got me set up, and I spent the night there. From then on, his mother called me her tenant.

◈ **The last time we'd had dinner together at our house, it was a Passover seder. Usually Easter and Passover coincide, and the Senate breaks for recess, but not this time, so we hadn't been able to make it back to New Haven. I'd almost invited other friends to join the Gores and us, and I'd almost hired someone to help in the kitchen. But then I'd realized that if I did, it wouldn't be the personal evening we wanted it to be, so I decided to keep it simple—and ask the Second Lady to join me on kitchen duty. She loved it. When you're the wife of the vice president, you don't get many chances to putter around a kitchen with a friend (and without some sort of staff listening in!).**

Here, at the Loews Hotel, the atmosphere was relaxed, with the easiness of a family dinner—except that one friend had just named the other friend his running mate in a presidential election, and none of us were going to be allowed to worry about the dishes.

◘ As we sat down to dinner, Al asked me to say grace, which I did gladly, thanking God for the opportunity I'd been given and asking God's blessing on both families as we went forward to Election Day. It was a good dinner, full of warm chatter and plans for the future. The Gores' son Albert and daughter Sarah were there. So were our son Matt and his wife, April. Matt had met April when they both were at Yale Law School, but she's originally from Gleason, a small town in the same western Tennessee county as the hometown of Al's mother, Pauline, so there was a lot of teasing back and forth about the local connections. To say nothing of the fact that the name of their first child, my first granddaughter, was Tennessee Lieberman, because April's family has a tradition that if a family member moves away from the state, they name a child after home.

Since Al Gore is from Carthage, Tennessee, the next day at the rally, I cracked, "Al, I want to thank you for mentioning my granddaughter Tennessee. I'm just sorry that we also couldn't be joined here by my cousin Carthage."

The Gores had figured out that Hani was the same age as Sarah had been when Al first ran for VP, so they sat the girls together. Sarah was at Harvard then, but she remembered 1992 vividly, and she was very comforting to Hani, who was excited but also in a state of shock. (Hani's got a good strong sense of privacy. In fact, I think she was secretly hoping I *wouldn't* be picked.)

55

I'm sitting there, looking around the table. There's Baba (which is what we call Joe's mother), and she's chatting with the vice president. Joe looks so happy. Matt and April are so excited, and our son Ethan and his wife, Ariela, are on their way; so is our daughter Rebecca. Matt and Becca are children of Joe's first marriage, Ethan is the child of my first marriage, and Hani was born to Joe and me, but in my heart and in Joe's there are no distinctions. These are *our* children, this is *our* family, and my heart is full.

And I think, Look at me, the daughter of Holocaust survivors. An immigrant. When you are an immigrant, you spend years trying to fit in—with language, with dress, but you always feel a little bit different. But here I am, with the vice president of the United States, and in a few months my husband, whom I love so much, may become the next vice president. The first Jewish vice president this country has ever had. (Later someone told me I was the first foreign-born spouse of a major party's candidate for national office since John Quincy Adams, whose wife was born in England.)

The feeling swept over me; I felt it, the excitement, but also the responsibility to bear witness at that moment. It was historic. Forget where the campaign might go. The fact was that we had already gotten to this point. We were there, in that room, and I was married to this wonderful man.

I think that I often take my family by surprise when I

speak. They're never quite sure what I'm going to say. I don't always know myself. This time I think I *really* surprised them, but I was driven to do it. I raised my glass and said, "I want to toast you, Mr. Vice President."

I turned and looked right into his eyes. "I want to toast you, because here I am, the daughter of Holocaust survivors and married to the man you have picked to be your vice presidential nominee. And I want to salute you and thank you for this great honor, and thank you for bringing me and my husband and our family to this exciting moment."

The room got very quiet. Al was obviously listening, and he said, "I won't forget what you said, Hadassah."

When the dinner was over, we said good night to our families, and Al, Tipper, Hadassah, and I went off to a meeting with the newly combined campaign staff. Very early the next morning, Al and I did the morning television shows from the roof of the Loews.

The overnight response to my selection was, as Kiki had said, beyond all expectations. Al was getting tremendous credit for being courageous and independent. What was particularly gratifying for me was that, while the headlines played up the barrier that was breaking, the coverage ultimately focused on how I had conducted my life. In other words, it was as much about who I was as about what I was.

◈ When we read the morning papers and saw how favorable they were to Joe, I thought about that scene in *Huckleberry Finn* when Huck is presumed "drownded" and he gets to listen to the eulogies at his funeral. The headline for the editorial in *The Washington Post* was INTEGRITY ON THE TICKET, and *The New York Times* praised Joe's "gravity and rectitude." I liked what George Will wrote. He called Joe "a practicing grown-up—the thinking person's choice." And I will always remember what *Washington Post* columnist Richard Cohen wrote. At first, his column seemed to be about our religious observances, but it ended up being about something even more fundamental than that:

"Not so long ago, Senator Joseph Lieberman and his wife, Hadassah, held a Friday night dinner party. By the time the Senate adjourned, the winter's sun had set and the Jewish Sabbath had begun. Lieberman, an Orthodox Jew, will not drive on the Sabbath. So with his guests waiting, he set out for home by foot, about five miles in the bitter cold. As with much else he set out to do in life, Lieberman got where he had to go no matter what. I tell you this story because I see it as being not about religious zealotry but about fidelity to values—the quality that is most mentioned when Lieberman's name comes up. Some call him sanctimonious and some call him moralistic, but everyone realizes that, in the end, this is a politician with a very demanding constituency: his conscience."

⧈ After we'd made our morning television appearances, Al and I went to work on our speeches for the announcement rally later that day at the War Memorial Plaza. At one point, Al looked up and asked, "Do you think Hadassah would be comfortable if we asked her to speak today?"

I said I didn't think it would be a problem.

"Well," he said, "do you think she would be comfortable sharing some of what she said at the table last night?"

"I think so, but why don't you ask her yourself?"

When Hadassah emerged (*not* at 5:00 A.M.) to wish us a good morning, Al asked her.

◈ I was surprised but flattered that what I had said in a private moment, something that came from my heart, was being seen as something that could be shared with all.

"Well, yes, of course," I told Al, because even though I felt anxious about speaking, I also felt empowered by his asking me. I felt empowered as a woman, and as the candidate's wife, but especially empowered as a child of survivors and as an immigrant. I could see why Al Gore wanted me to speak. He knew that I could stand there and represent the American dream. I could truthfully say to all immigrants, to every American who might feel different, This land is our land, we can rise here. Our family has. You all can.

◈ A little later, we had a briefing and a run-through before the rally. Tipper was to introduce Hadassah and then introduce Al, who would in turn introduce his new running mate to the crowd. There were about twenty people at the run-through, and when it was over, Hadassah walked to the podium and started studying and annotating her stack of three-by-five cards, on which she had written notes for her short speech. I looked over and saw that Al had gone to her side. "Now, Hadassah," he was saying quietly, "I was thinking you might want to try it this way." Very gently, protectively, the vice president was coaching my wife on her first national speech.

The heat was brutal and the humidity smothering, but still there were almost ten thousand people at the War Memorial to cheer us on. *The New York Times* the next day would call it a "boisterous gathering," and it was indeed. A joyous choir, drenched in sweat, sang out "God Bless America." Someone read the Tennessee State poem. The immensely popular Jewel, under usual conditions a lovely, gentle spirit, was clearly uncomfortable as she played her guitar and treated the crowd to a few of her hits. "My Alaskan blood isn't doing too good out here," complained the singer-songwriter, who had been raised in Homer, Alaska. "It is *hot.*" She yodeled her way through a song her father had taught her, and then she was gone. It was our turn.

The four of us swept onto the stage, and the crowd erupted in cheers. It was pure joy. As the sun beat down on us, Al and I peeled off our jackets and stood in our white shirts.

"Joe and I come from different regions and different religious faiths," Al told the crowd, "but we believe in a common set of ideals, and we both believe with our whole resolve that, as Americans, we must make real the great ideal that we are one country with a common destiny.

"Next week, when our party meets in Los Angeles, we will recall the last time we met there, at the convention where we nominated John F. Kennedy. That year we voted with our hearts to make history by tearing down an old wall of division, and when we nominate Joe Lieberman for vice president, we will make history again. We will tear down an old wall of division once again."

When I spoke, I gave Al the credit he deserved. "Let's be very clear about this—let's be very clear about this; it isn't me, Joe Lieberman, who deserves the credit and the congratulations for taking a bold step, it is Al Gore who broke this barrier in American history!" I said. "Now, my friends, I stand here today with a proud, simple, but I think, very important message: Al Gore of Tennessee is the best man to lead America into the new century!"

I loved the cheering crowd, and the crowd returned that love. But I think the person who stole their hearts that day was Hadassah.

◈ All of a sudden I understood: Okay, Joe is the VP candidate, and this is a historic moment, but I won't be speaking for him or for me only, because this is beyond either of us. I am here to represent the immigrants who made it here, and another group, too: the *neshomas,* the souls that hadn't made it.

Memories I had inherited from my parents taught me about what it's like to be a pariah and victim. They came out of a time period when Jews felt apart, alone, downtrodden, and distraught. But we did survive, and for that I have the American GIs to thank, and I needed to thank them and pay tribute to them.

"Here I am," I said, "in this place that commemorates World War Two . . . and here I am, the daughter of survivors from the Holocaust, the most horrendous things that happened, and here I am in the place that commemorates the American heroes, the soldiers who actually liberated my mother from Dachau and Auschwitz, and so I stand before you very deeply, sincerely thankful that I am an American; grateful that we have such a wonderful, wonderful family and friends in the Gores, and that they've made this bold, wonderful choice to help us be part of the ticket that's going to win!

"Let me end now with just this one statement, and I say this to all of you here and all of you who are watching this on television, and this is real:

"Whether you or your family emigrated from Europe,

Africa, Mexico, Latin America, or Asia, I am standing here for you! This country is our country! This land is your land, and anything is possible for us!"

⧈ Hadassah spoke with sincerity and passion, and I looked at our children, and they all had tears in their eyes, and then I looked out at the cheering crowd and realized that many had tears in their eyes, too. This was not your run-of-the-mill political speech making. This was something very genuine and very moving.

◈ I spoke from my heart. When we came to America, the only language I could speak was Yiddish. That was true until I began school, and then I said I would speak only English. I didn't want to be different anymore, even though, in some ways, because of my background, I always would be different. But I wanted to be an American like everyone else.

In the campaign, something amazing happened. I talked about the fact that I was an immigrant and how that not only connected me in a very personal way with other immigrants but also seemed to make me more American.

When I went down the rope line after that speech, people grabbed me and pulled me close to them. There

were immigrants from all over and older military veterans wiping away tears. It was an amazing moment. I was overcome. I wish my brave and remarkable mother could have been there with me, but she was too frail to leave her home in Riverdale, New York, that day.

Still, she got to watch me on television, and a *New York Times* reporter watched with her. "I haven't slept in two days already, just answering congratulations," my mother told the reporter. "I haven't eaten today. I am just sitting and crying."

CHAPTER FIVE

It is conventional wisdom that there are three critical moments in a vice presidential campaign: the announcement of your selection, your convention speech, and the vice presidential debate. Those are the pivotal times when a vice presidential nominee can really add or subtract from a campaign.

The announcement had gone as beautifully as anyone could have dared dream. Tom Nides said, "It was quite astonishing; raw jubilation," and enthusiasm for the ticket just kept building. Bill Daley, who was campaign chairman, called it "Liebermania," and he said, "The reaction to Lieberman has been about as good as you could hope for leading up to the convention. In a lot of ways, it has really changed the dynamic of the convention."

The Republicans got the expected substantial boost from their convention in Philadelphia the week before, but now one poll showed our ticket going from seventeen points down to only two points behind, literally overnight. It was essential that our convention move us ahead and into the fall campaign with momentum.

The best way I could help make that happen was by giving a great speech. It would have to be substantial and inspirational. I wanted it to be biographical but not boring, and patriotic but not patronizing.

I've learned something about myself as a speaker over the years. Although I am certainly not a latter-day William Jennings Bryan, I can get fired up and give a pretty good political speech. But I am at my most effective when I have a message and ideas that are mine and that I can therefore deliver with conviction. Many people in the campaign would be commenting on this speech as it was being drafted, so I knew I needed to work hard to make sure it ended up as my thoughts in my voice.

An enormous amount of activity and stress attends the drafting of a speech as important as this one. And while a presidential candidate usually has many weeks to prepare for the convention, a vice presidential candidate has, well, in this case, roughly a week. I've had only three real speechwriters during my career, and each of them had the time to get to know me. Paul Orzulak never had that luxury, but on the plane to Nashville that first day, he just sat down and asked me about my life and my beliefs, and he did it again later in the week on another flight. He was looking and listening for ideas and experiences that were mine that he could put in the two important speeches he would swiftly have to draft—the announcement speech, followed by the acceptance speech.

We had a first draft ready by the Sunday before the Democratic National Convention, which was set to start the next day, August 14, in Los Angeles. I was scheduled to speak Wednesday night. On that Sunday, Paul, Jonathan Sallet, and I worked over the draft at my home in Georgetown. The next morning, we brought in more people—Bill Bonvillian, Bill Andresen, and Dan Gerstein of my Senate staff—who helped us develop the speech.

Monday afternoon, Hadassah and I start making our way to Los Angeles. First we stop in St. Louis near the arch for an outdoor rally with the Gores. That night we have dinner in their hotel room, and together we watch the opening night of the convention. Television and still photographers are let in for a while to watch us watch TV.

This is President Clinton's night. Since the networks will go to local news at 11:00 (eastern time), the president must be on by 10:30. But the earlier speakers are going too long, and Al calls someone backstage in Los Angeles to urge them to speed it up. Hillary Clinton comes to the podium around 10:30, and President Clinton doesn't start speaking until 10:55. But the networks decide to stick with him, leading the Republicans to claim that this was all a plot by us to get more airtime. I wish. The president is very gracious to Al and me in his speech. When he finishes, Al immediately has a call put through to the president (a new telecommunications experience for me), and we both congratulate him on a great job. Then Hadassah and I leave for the St. Louis airport, climb onto our small plane, and fly to Los Angeles, arriving at two in the morning. To our surprise and delight, we are greeted by Bob Hertzberg, the impressive Speaker of the California State Assembly, and a hearty group of Democrats.

The next morning, the Gore consultants weigh in with their opinions about my speech. Pollster Stan Greenberg is with us; also by phone, are strategists Bob Shrum and Carter Eskew, who received the text the day before.

The irony is that, after all the involvement by so many others, I wind up with a speech that is probably more personal than any I've ever given. On the plane to Nashville, I had told Paul Orzulak about my college years, about marching with Martin Luther King and signing up voters in Mississippi. In my entire political career in Connecticut, I don't think I ever mentioned the fact that I worked in the civil rights movement. It just seemed like a small personal piece of something very big long ago. But Paul put my recollections of it into this speech. I also told Paul about my dad and the fact that he had spent part of his childhood in an orphanage and started his first job working on a bakery truck, and that too is included.

Earlier in the process I asked Jonathan Sallet, "What should be the organizing principle of my speech?"

"*You* are the organizing principle," he said.

In fact, the text is so autobiographical that I wonder whether I am overdoing it. But then I realize that it is ultimately not about me. My history is part of the story, but the speech is really about the greatness of this country. It's about opportunity. It's about the opportunity every kid in America should have to realize his or her dream. It's about the fact that here I am, the first person in my family to go to college. Here I am, married to a woman whose parents survived unspeakable horrors to settle here, where they found a welcoming home. What the speech says is what I deeply believe: that this is a great country, yet as good as things are today, working together, with the right kind of leadership, we can make it better. The best is yet to come.

◈ Tuesday afternoon arrives and Joe is scheduled to have a run-through with the TelePrompTer. But Nashville has just faxed in more last minute "suggestions," and we don't have a revised text to practice with yet. Jon Sallet tries to break the news gently. He says, "Uh, Senator, we're in great shape, really, just great shape . . . there's just one small problem . . ."

He was *terrified* that Joe would explode. So was Tom Nides. See, these people hadn't worked with Joe long enough to know that he doesn't explode. And he wasn't worried. He knew that if he had a copy of the speech by

the end of the day, he could spend the next day practicing and he'd be fine.

⧈ I also knew that this would give me a last chance to ensure that all the words were mine. I like to write, and I have a strong sense of what I want to say. I know that I'm the one up there speaking. I am the one who's going to be judged by the speech. I want the words to be mine.

◈ Later, Jon and Tom both told me that when they told friends about how calm Joe had been about the missing speech, their friends were completely in awe. Jon said, "One of them said, 'That is amazing. If I hadn't had a speech ready for my boss, he'd have thrown me right *through* the wall.'"

Joe's speech may not have been ready for loading into the TelePrompTer, but mine was. Tipper was going to introduce Al at the convention, and I was going to introduce Joe. So it was time for practice. This was the first time I had ever read off a TelePrompTer—and I found the whole thing impossible. The TelePrompTer was an impediment to my spontaneity. My ease in public speaking totally disappeared as eyes from around the room peered at me, analyzing every movement,

each pause. How can I be me? How can I say what I want to say? I kept tripping over the words:

> It's hard to believe that it was only one week ago that Tipper and I were in my wonderful hometown, Gardner, Massachusetts, to celebrate this newest adventure in our lives. To all of our family, our old friends, our new friends, we thank you. We thank you for your support, for your enthusiasm, for your love. It has been overwhelming, and so gratifying. Tonight I want to share with you some very personal thoughts about my Joey.

My brother, Ary, was there, and he remembers how painful it was: "In Hadassah's first efforts, she became tongue-tied and made several significant reading errors. The second and third tries were even worse, but the text was great."

> For Joe, family, faith, neighborhood, congregation, and community are the guideposts of his life, orienting the choices he makes and the causes that he champions. Community keeps Joe grounded and reminds him of his commitment to respectful living. It reminds him to embrace our nation's diversity and to celebrate our differences. It reminds him of the Republic he serves: One nation under God, indivisible, with liberty and justice for all.

"By the time we finished," Ary recalls, "after about ten tries, she had failed to provide a single reading without serious errors, leaving her flustered and anxious. I didn't think she was going to be able to handle the speech—for whatever reason. I debated with myself whether to advise her to call it quits and let someone else make the introduction, hoping to spare her a humiliation, but I was fearful of raising her level of anxiety. In the end, I decided that it was her night and that, whatever the results, she was entitled to the experience."

Listen, about this Lieberman . . . he really hates Hollywood violence, doesn't he? . . . I hear he wants to censor out the dog's death in Old Yeller *and the sled-burning in* Citizen Kane *. . . He probably covers his eyes in* The Wizard of Oz *when the witch melts.*

—Mike Downey in the *Los Angeles Times,* August 20, 2000

Los Angeles had not hosted the Democratic National Convention since 1960, when John F. Kennedy was nominated, and the city was ready for it. But was Hollywood ready for me?

MOGULS RATTLED BY GORE'S CHOICE. That was the headline of a *New York Times* article, which reported: "The entertainment industry is facing the Democratic National Convention here next week with some last-minute jitters. Vice President Al Gore's choice of Senator Joseph I. Lieberman as his running mate has chilled wealthy Hollywood Democrats, who are upset that Mr. Lieberman is one of the Senate's most vocal critics of Hollywood."

I had led hearings on violence in video games. I had teamed up with my conservative Republican friend Bill Bennett to crusade against violent and sexually explicit entertainment. Back in May, I had joined Arizona senator John McCain and two other colleagues in a letter asking the Federal Communications Commission (FCC) to push the broadcast industry harder in policing themselves.

The press was quick to point out that some of these very people had contributed generously in recent years to the Democratic Party. Over his eight years as president, Clinton developed a close relationship with many of the leaders of the entertainment industry, and as a result, they had been very supportive of the party. By the start of the convention, the entertainment industry had become the fourth most generous backer to the Democratic National Committtee in 2000, donating $6 million.

There were a few Democratic fund-raising types who hoped I would pull my punches, mute my criticism, but I wasn't about to do that. Al Gore said to me during a flight on Air Force Two that week, "I chose you because of who you are, so don't let anyone change you." The Sunday before the start of the convention, I made the rounds on the talk shows and continued to spell out my grave concerns about the entertainment industry. "I continue to believe, though I love the movies and the entertainment media, that too much of what comes out is too full of violence and sex and incivility, and it is bad for our children," I told CBS's *Face the Nation,* repeating views I had been expressing for nearly a decade. I didn't want, have never wanted, governmental censorship, I said, but I did feel—and continue to feel very strongly—that we need to lean on the industry to self-regulate.

Heading into the convention, Gore apparently called a few friends in the entertainment industry and discussed his choice with them, and there wasn't much concern. For the most part, industry leaders recognized that this wasn't a one-issue campaign. As Rob Reiner told a *Washington Post* reporter, "I'm not really concerned about Hollywood's parochial interests." He said the industry issues are "minuscule" compared with education, health care, and the environment. Most people, in fact, took a position similar to the one Jeffrey Katzenberg, one of the founders of DreamWorks SKG and a close friend of Clinton's, articulated to *The New York Times:* "Yes, Lieberman has been critical, and held us in Hollywood to a very high standard. It's not something we have often agreed upon in terms of the solution. But to have someone as direct and honest and doesn't pull punches is what leadership is all about."

If you want a complete historical picture of the 2000 Democratic National Convention, you will have to consult some other account, because large parts of the convention are just a blur to Hadassah and me. It comes back to us in pieces and flashes. The entire family, gathered backstage for a group photo, spontaneously bursting into "God Bless America" at the top of our lungs. Was that before I gave my acceptance speech or after? Was it Wednesday or Thursday night? "The Blue Team" in action—Tipper Gore in her sky blue dress and Hillary Rodham Clinton in a cornflower blue suit, and Hadassah Freilich Lieberman, radiant in hyacinth (I learned the colors from *The New York Times,* which quoted a fashion person as saying, "Blue is soothing but powerful"). Glancing down as a crowd chanted, "Go, Joe, go!" and seeing my eighty-five-year-old mother beam back.

Tuesday late afternoon, Pacific coast time. We've been underneath the floor of the convention hall, practicing my speech in the room with the mock podium and TelePrompTer, and someone decides the delegates are getting listless. So they ask me to go out onto the convention floor. From the soft quiet of backstage, I enter the hall through a door in the back, and suddenly there's a burst of frenetic jubilation. They call it "Liebermania." I'm getting crushed; security surrounds me. It's my Elvis moment. People are grabbing me to hug me and kiss me and shake my hand. Somebody tells me to get up on a chair and wave to the crowd, and as I do, the enormous crowd roars, and I can feel this rush of excitement and acceptance and warmth and optimism. As my children describe it, this is the closest I'll ever come to diving into a mosh pit. When I come back to quiet offstage, I say, "That was *incredible*! When can I do it again?!"

That night, while Hadassah and I try to get some sleep, our children—the newest "pseudocelebrities," as Matt put it—head out on the town. Becca delights in meeting *Seinfeld*'s Julia Louis-Dreyfus at the Schwarzenegger-Shriver party, while her sister, Hana, chats with CNN anchor Judy Woodruff and her husband, *Wall Street Journal* columnist Al Hunt.

"It was so, so cool," says Hana.

"Hmmm . . . one of us seems to be more substantive," says Becca.

"What do you expect?" says Matt. "Hani grew up mostly as a Beltway kid."

The next night, at the Sunset Club, Sheryl Crow updates another great American moment by serenading Matt with a breathy version of "Happy Birthday . . . Mr. Son of the Vice President." He is turning thirty-three.

From *The Secret*
by Matthew Lieberman

L.A.

Convention, confusion
Pseudo-celebrity

Walking down Sunset Boulevard like we said we would,
Tan, smiling, arm in arm, suited up, a Hollywood
swagger . . .
We go to any party we want.
Because we're it.
The Big "It."
The famous people no one knows.
And the California stars twinkle down upon us.
Martin Sheen, the President, overjoyed to see us, and
his wife
Very nice people.
And Josh Lyman and Leo McGarry and Donna and Toby
The whole West Wing, even Charlie, happy to meet us.
And Sean Penn, all in black.
And my pal Jimmy Smits.
And Jesse Jackson pulling me into the next box
Where Cher is,
Because he has an important message to give my father.
And Timmy, JFK's nephew, coming to the family box to
say Hi.
And a staff person looking at me to check
Is he o.k.?
We're having a little party, he says,
A scrap of yellow paper;
A cell phone number;
Party at Maria and Arnold's
Yes, I think we can make that.
And a living room, conjured and sprawled across a
wide lawn

And food and the famous.
And our handlers handling us around
To Maria and cousin Caroline
To Brokaw and Williams and Russert and Barnicle
To Lauren Bacall and Carl Lewis and Elaine Benes
And Ali's manager—"anything I can do."
To millions here and billions there
And a bridge over a moat
And Arnold now here, now inside
Entertaining a small group late in the evening.
Cigars and Warhols.
Away
And on to
Another party—I can't remember.
Maybe, but quite a day.

◈ Wednesday, August 16. At 10:00 P.M. on the nose, Hadassah walks out onto the stage of the Staples Center. *Hadassah! Hadassah! Hadassah!* Her brother, Ary, and dear friend Mindy Weisel brace themselves. "My anxiety level was very, very high," Ary says. But love and excitement from the crowd sweep up onto the stage, and "in a matter of seconds," he says, "when Hadassah clasped her hands to her heart in response to the roars of the crowd, I immediately knew she was in control, comfortable in her element, and about to create a magical moment. And she did."

Hadassah introduces her "Joey" at the Los Angeles convention.

Some folks have said my husband is just a regular Joe. He is that, and he's much more. His connection to the larger community has molded a vision that is anything but ordinary. When Al Gore chose my husband as his running mate, this country got a man whose mission in life is inspired by the people, the people that he serves and the community he loves.

Ladies and gentlemen, it gives me great, great pleasure to introduce my husband, my best friend, and the love of my life, Joe Lieberman.

◘ Mindy and Ary are crying. The delegates are pumped up, and I am ready. The orchestra breaks into the triumphant theme from the movie *Chariots of Fire.* In 1982 my staff had it played when I was nominated to be state attorney general. I wasn't there, because the state convention was taking place on a Saturday—and my staff picked the music because the movie was about a devout Christian athlete who refused to compete on Sundays.

LIEBERMAN: Is America a great country or what?! (Cheers, applause.) Yes it is! God bless America, land that we love!

Dear friends, ten days ago, with courage and with friendship, Al Gore asked me to be his running mate. (Cheers, applause.) And I don't have to tell you that this has been a most extraordinary week for my family and me.

There's an old saying that behind every successful man, there's a surprised mother-in-law. (Laughter.) Well, I can tell you that this week, that's been particularly true. (Laughter.)

[A] miraculous journey begins here and now. Tonight, I am so proud to stand as your candidate for vice president of the United States. (Cheers, applause.)

AUDIENCE: Joe. Joe. Joe. Joe. Joe. Joe.

LIEBERMAN: Only in America, right? (Cheers, applause.) Only in America.

AUDIENCE: We want Joe. We want Joe. We want Joe.

"It feels monumental and momentous," Becca recalls. "I look down, and there are members of the Connecticut delegation whom we've known for years, and they are crying. It is heartwarming but it is also astonishing. We're amazed by this enormous shift in the public role of our father, and I know this sounds strange, but you stand there and you almost feel you're losing custody of your dad."

◈ **Joe was at his best that night, and I was not the only one who thought so. No less an authority than *The Washington Post*'s David S. Broder called the speech "alternately personal, passionate and funny. . . ." It was, he wrote, "a hit." Someone told us George Stephanopoulos said on ABC something like "At each national conven-**

A very happy warrior addresses the Democratic National Convention in Los Angeles, August 2000.

tion, a star is born. That is what happened to Joe Lieberman tonight."

> As I stand here before you tonight, blessed to have the opportunity I have, I know that we have become the America that so many of our parents dreamed for us. But the great question this year is what will we dream for our country, and how will we make it come true? We who gather here tonight believe, as Al Gore has said, that it's not just the size of our national feast that's important, no, but the number of people we can fit around the table. There must be room for everybody! . . .

And then I set out some of the themes I would return to repeatedly during the campaign: the extraordinary accomplishments of the Clinton-Gore administration, twenty-two million new jobs, a hard-earned national surplus, reduced rates of crime, welfare reform, environmental protection, and a strong military. ("Our fighting men and women are the best-trained, best-equipped, most potent fighting force in the history of the world.")

I also describe the concerns Al and I share about our popular culture:

> Long before it became popular, Al and Tipper led a crusade to renew the moral center of this nation. . . . He knows that in many Americans there is a swelling sense that our standards of decency and civility have eroded. It's

just this simple: No parent should be forced to compete with popular culture to raise their children.

I had introduced myself, praised Gore, criticized Bush (particularly his record in Texas), and advanced my kind of New Democratic policies. Now it was time to close in terms that were, at once, historical and yet very personal.

It was forty years ago when we came to this city, and together crossed a New Frontier, with a leader who inspired me and so many others in my generation into public service.

Today we return to this same great city, with prosperity at home and freedom throughout the world that John F. Kennedy could only have dreamed about.

We may wonder tonight where the next frontier really is. Tonight, I believe the next frontier isn't just in front of us, but inside of us: to overcome the differences that are still between us, to break down the barriers that remain, and to help every American claim the possibilities of their own God-given lives.

You know, sometimes I try to see this world as my dad saw it from that bakery truck. Right about this time of day, he'd be getting ready for the all-night run. And I know that somewhere in America right now, there's another father loading another bakery truck, or a young woman programming a computer, or a parent dreaming of a better future for their daughter or their son. My friends, if we keep the faith, then forty years from now, one of their

After the nominations.

children will stand before a gathering like this, as I am tonight, with the chance that I have to serve and lead this great country that we love so dearly. That's what America is about.

So, let us work together to make sure that they will be able to look back to this time and this stage and this place and say of our generation, "They kept the faith."

Let them say that we helped them realize their hopes and their dreams. And let them look around at this great and good nation that we are all so blessed by God to share, and say, "Only in America."

CHAPTER SIX

One morning on the campaign trail, I woke up in Little Rock, Arkansas. Hadassah was on the road, too, off in Minneapolis, Minnesota, and I missed her, so I gave her an early call in her hotel room before our days began and got too crazy.

Hadassah sounded upbeat. "Things are good," she assured me. "In fact, there is a wonderful story about me on the front page of the *Minneapolis Star Tribune* this morning. Nice picture, too."

"Isn't that great," I responded. And then one of those awful competitive genes got moving in me, and I said, "Incidentally, sweetheart, there is a very nice picture of me on the front page of the *Little Rock Democrat Gazette* this morning."

Hadassah paused for exactly the right amount of time and then asked coolly: "Are you above the fold?"

I wasn't. She was. Case closed.

◈ I knew the rules. I was a soldier in a national campaign. I was particularly aware that the role of the spouse of the vice presidential candidate is to support both her spouse and the presidential nominee. But sometimes I'd get out there and look around the room and the text of the speech just felt like a distraction. And even though I'd have these people in my ear all the time saying, "It's important to win people over on this point. You've got to make that point," some days that just wasn't enough. You are having this natural, honest response, this back-and-forth transaction with people—and the script would frustrate me, hold me back. It's always my instinct to talk directly to the people. That's what I *like* to do. I don't want the podium and microphone to be a barrier.

So I'd get out there and look around the room, and I'd say, "Now listen. I have a speech here that I'm supposed to give to you, but you know what? I just want to talk to you instead. I want to talk to you, and listen and answer your questions, all right?" At that moment my staff was probably annoyed that once again I had ignored the prepared remarks. But the crowds would respond. People were hungry for direct communication, for realness. It was amazing to feel the palpable response. Here we were in the midst of the largest rallies, and I always felt the people's arms and eyes and voices reaching out to touch the candidates and their spouses.

◘ When the trips were over, I'd hear Hadassah's staff report, "My God, people were so into her!" I knew that was the truth, and I also knew why it was happening. It's because Hadassah was speaking from her heart.

It took just one speech under the baking sun of Nashville, and Hadassah had become a personality. When she was introduced at the War Memorial Plaza, the MC couldn't pronounce her name—he punched the first syllable, "HAH-da-sa." That wasn't a problem for long. Soon I was boasting to crowds that my wife had entered "a very select group of women who are known by only their first name—like Oprah or Madonna."

If you ask our children what was the most moving moment at the Democratic National Convention, it was when the floor of the convention hall turned into a sea of blue and white "Hadassah" signs. "That was the most amazing thing," says Hani, and it was. It was amazing, too, to hear thousands of men and women chant my wife's name. (Correctly.)

It's a wonderful name, a biblical name. In Hebrew, it means "myrtle." It's also the Hebrew equivalent of Esther, originally a Persian name, from the biblical story of Queen Esther, who saved her people by intervening with the king. My Hadassah's father wanted to give her the name Esther for her maternal grandmother, who had been killed in the Holocaust. For some reason, the Czech authorities felt the name sounded German, so she was given the Hebrew equivalent—Hadassah. When the family came to this country and settled in Gardner, Massachusetts, he wanted to switch back to Esther. It sounded more American. But when he filled out the citizenship paper listing "Esther" as his daughter, the Catholic nun helping process the naturalization papers stopped him. "Oh, don't do that," she said. "Hadassah is such a beautiful name, and it's from the Bible. Keep it." God bless that sister.

◈ You're moving so fast in a campaign like this, you lose your sense of reality. You don't know where you are—and sometimes who you are. You don't know what hotel you're in; you never go through a main entrance. Your life swarms in all directions. And every time you try to reach your husband the candidate, he's knee deep in other people.

After thirteen years of campaigns, I thought I knew what a campaign schedule looked like. But this was different—very different. This schedule was like riding an unstoppable roller coaster wearing a very tight seat belt. October 17:

10:45 a.m.	Wheels down in Albuquerque, NM
10:50 a.m.	Arrival airport meet and greet to thank local supporters
11:00 a.m.	Depart for health care event
11:35 a.m.	Health care roundtable discussion at YWCA
12:00 p.m.	Proceed for press interview

12:05 p.m.	Interview w/ABC-TV affiliate
12:10 p.m.	Interview w/NBC-TV affiliate
12:15 p.m.	Interview w/CBS-TV affiliate
12:20 p.m.	Interview w/*Albuquerque Journal* political reporter (print)
12:25 p.m.	Interview w/*Albuquerque Tribune* political reporter (print)
12:30 p.m.	Interview with AP political reporter
12:35 p.m.	Depart YWCA
12:50 p.m.	Visit Barela's Coffee Shop to visit everyday voters and a local hot spot
1:00 p.m.	Depart for airport
1:20 p.m.	Board plane and taxi
1:30 p.m.	Wheels up
2:10 p.m.	Wheels down in Las Vegas

And we do it all over again. . . . I thought I was busy before the campaign. Ha! It's not just that every moment is scheduled—it's that you are absorbing everything, learning, feeling it all.

They said I could make a difference. So I tried, but because you're in such a cocoon, it's difficult to know what sort of impact you're having; you have to wait until somebody reads you your press.

⊡ A national campaign is so all-consuming that you have to take a big part of your normal life and turn it over to other people. After I was selected, I signed a book of blank checks and handed them over to my former executive assistant, Carleen Overstreet Morris, who paid all my bills from August through December. Our older children, Matt, Becca, and Ethan were off on their own, but our twelve-year-old, Hani, needed support and supervision. So my mom, when she wasn't out campaigning herself, and our dear friend Susanne Brose moved into our house in Washington. Technology bridged the space between normal life and campaign life, as when Hani faxed me her English homework somewhere out there in America, and as is our custom, I edited and commented on it; then I faxed it back. Our neighbors had to adjust, too. Two big Secret Service trailers parked on our street, and there was a constant presence of agents around the house. Locks were changed, new phones installed. All our friends, even our neighbors, the Leval family, whose three daughters had gone to school with Hani for the past nine years, had to first "check in" at the door with the agents before dropping in.

I remember so well our first Friday out on the campaign trail. The convention was over. In an incredible final night, Al had given a rousing acceptance speech and we all celebrated at a gala star-studded fund-raiser at the Los Angeles theater where the Academy Awards used to be held. Then, in a burst of adrenaline, we boarded a plane and flew overnight to La Crosse, Wisconsin—the first stop of what was to be a four-day riverboat and bus trip down the Mississippi, through America's heartland. Now we were out on the campaign trail, and we were back to the real world, going down one of America's most beautiful rivers, rich with history and lore, and we were with the kinds of mainstream people who are the heart and soul of America. It felt wonderful.

Not too many years ago, the weeks following the conventions were relatively quiet, a getting-to-know-you period for the campaign staffs. Campaigns didn't really kick off until Labor Day. Bill Clinton helped change all that. Immediately after his first convention in 1992, Bill and Hillary Clinton and Al and Tipper Gore took off on a bus tour of more than one thousand miles of the USA. The Democratic ticket was young, vital, of the people, and out with the people.

The Clinton-Gore bus trip in 1992 was such a success, it set a new standard for future campaigns. After he was nominated, George W. Bush climbed on a train and chugged around Pennsylvania, Ohio, Michigan, and Illinois. Less than two weeks later, we were aboard the riverboat *Mark Twain*.

The boat offered us gorgeous views of Wisconsin's hills to the east and the bluffs of Minnesota to the west, and the river provided us with a metaphor; a banner draped over the side proclaimed, "Setting Course for America's Future." More pragmatically, it also gave us access to four battleground states—Wisconsin, Iowa, Illinois, and Missouri. That's 51 electoral votes of the 270 needed to win.

Each day, we'd make three or four stops along the riverbank; sometimes we'd welcome people aboard for a town hall–style meeting or policy discussion; other times we would go off the boat to walk along the banks talking with people or to go to a rally in town. We'd start by reminding our audiences of the strong economy, and as I said to someone along the way, what could be more evocative of good times than a sunny summer day on a riverboat? We'd then dive into specifics on such issues as health care, education, and the environment. We'd talk about tax cuts, paying down the national debt, prescription drugs for seniors, and a patients' bill of rights.

"Do you want to know the facts?" Gore would yell to the crowds. And they'd yell back, "Yes!"

"Am I giving you too many specifics?" he'd ask. And they'd call back, "No!"

As one of the consultants told a reporter for the *Los Angeles Times,* "The more we get specific, the less the other guy looks specific."

These were great days. The crowds were in the thousands and enthusiastic, and the dynamic between Hadassah and me and the Gores worked very well. It wasn't manufactured. We knew and liked one another. And we developed a regular order to these joint appearances. It began with Hadassah, who introduced Tipper, who introduced me, who introduced "the next president of the United States." The campaign managers called these joint appearances "double-dating," and it would have been great if we'd been able to keep traveling together. But that was hardly a practical way to run a campaign that was so close in so many states. If you divide a national election into fifty contests (which, really, is what you must do with the electoral college), you have to look at the campaign as fifty individual elections. You need to spread out the candidates and their wives and other surrogates and have each cover different states almost every day.

From the start, the campaign managers had counted on using Tipper, who's a wonderful and experienced campaigner. But they also realized that Hadassah had overnight become a force. They needed to put her to work.

In the War Room at the headquarters in Nashville, the campaign staff pored over the polling to decide where to send us. The ultimate goal, obviously, was to win enough states to get us to 270 electoral votes. But first you had to figure out what resources to commit to which states in order to reach that goal, and you needed to know how to, in a sense, *quantify and measure* your resources. To do that, campaign advisers devised a point system that worked like this: All of us—Al, Tipper, me, Hadassah, our kids—were assigned points. The more impact you were likely to have (the presidential nominee ranked tops), the higher the number assigned to you. So, for example, if I visited a state, that would count for two hundred points, whereas a visit from Hadassah would count for one hundred points. Second visits to a state counted for fewer points than a first visit. Paid commercials got points, as did free media such as a newscast, and so on.

Meanwhile, in Nashville, they would be analyzing: In

Our family. Front row: daughter Hana, Joe, and Hadassah. Back row: (left to right) daughter Rebecca, son Ethan, daughter-in-law Ariela Migdal, daughter-in-law April Lieberman, and son Matt Lieberman. The last night of the convention, Los Angeles.

this battleground state here, we'll need x number of points to tip the balance and win the state. And then they'd allocate enough resources to win. A visit from our kids was worth something, although they were down on the point scale, which Hadassah thought was very funny. She liked to remind them, "Hey, don't get so uppity. You're worth only fifty points, you know."

The truth is that our children were "worth" a lot more than fifty points. Matt and Becca stopped their normal lives, left their jobs, and spent the campaign on the road, usually alone, sometimes with Hadassah or me. Ethan, who was still at graduate school, and our daughters-in-law, April and Ariela, went out whenever they could. Only our twelve-year-old, Hani, stayed focused on her education. Hadassah and I still meet people all the time who tell us they saw our children during the campaign and thought they were great. They are.

◈ **It was just as well that I started feeling more comfortable about being on my "own" campaign trail, because more and more, Nashville was assigning me to go out on my own, to make appearances at rallies and fundraisers, to do a lot of my own media. But when you are the Second Lady nominee, you're always fighting an internal battle for resources and time and attention. You have a small staff, but then you're expected to travel all over the country, drop in on two or three cities a day,** and you're not flying on Air Force Two. You're at the mercy of commercial airlines. You're schlepping your luggage from terminal to terminal, praying that you see it come down the chute at the baggage claim.

Now you know, Tipper had been through this before. And at some point very late in the 1992 campaign, she had managed to get her own plane. It was nothing fancy, but it got her where she needed to go. Sally Aman, my campaign manager, is an old friend of Tipper's, dating back to her work on the 1992 campaign. So one day Sally and I were flying with Tipper, on her plane, to a campaign event, and Sally just happened to mention that things were getting pretty difficult for us, that increasing amounts of travel were being expected, but, you know what it's like, commercial flights aren't all that time-flexible, so we had to schedule our events around plane schedules or sometimes we missed planes altogether. We'd tried to get Nashville to give us a private plane, but they wouldn't.

Well, telling Tipper was all it took. She said, I'm going to tell Al that I'm not going travel anymore until you get a plane.

Of course, I said, Oh, no, no, Tipper, please don't worry about us, we'll be okay, I'm sure. . . . But at the same time, although Sally and I knew that Nashville wasn't going to be happy with us, we also knew that getting a plane was the only way to do the job they wanted us to do.

Tipper picked up the phone, told her husband what

she had told us, and hung up. The next day, Sally and I drove out to National Airport in Washington, D.C.—and boarded our own plane. It was small, but it was ours.

Soon Nashville had Hadassah flying all over the country, speaking before rallies and fund-raisers. Some in the campaign were surprised and impressed by her immediate ability to make genuine, emotional contact with people, whether in huge arenas or, quietly, one on one. But I wasn't surprised at all, because I live with her. I know her gifts, her genuineness, and her power. I remember that wonderful challenge in E. M. Forster's *Howards End:* "Only connect!" Wherever Hadassah goes, she connects.

People would wait for a glimpse of her, lining up for the airplanes to land in the morning, waving us off at night. Heather Picazio, from my Hartford U.S. Senate office staff, had been assigned to travel with Hadassah, and she vividly remembers this one "tiny old old" man in a "tiny" airport in Pennsylvania. "He was just sitting there," she said, "not moving, but looking as if he were waiting for something, someone. Finally, as we were about to board the plane, I walked up to him and said hello."

"Are you with Mrs. Lieberman?" he asked. And when Heather said yes, he told her he was ninety-six years old and that he had been waiting for two hours, hoping to have the chance to meet Hadassah. So of course she went to get Hadassah.

"What was so sweet," Heather said, "was that Hadassah kept sitting there with him, holding his hand with both of hers. Those few minutes meant everything to him because, he told her, he never could have imagined that a child of survivors could actually make it this far in this world."

That was typical of a very moving part of the campaign —the Holocaust survivors, waiting behind the rope lines, would roll up their sleeves and hold their arms to show the concentration camp numbers burned into their flesh. Our campaign meant so much to them, said so much to them about how far they had come from the horrors. "They just wanted to touch Hadassah," says Heather. When this happened, Hadassah would often lead them to the side so they could talk awhile. The survivors were so proud of her, they treated her like a daughter, and they'd invariably weep when they'd see her. "Oh, the crying!" Heather remembers. "The Secret Service used to joke about it. An agent would go away on shift rotation for three weeks, come back, and say, 'Oh, God, the crying is *still* going on!' "

But it wasn't only survivors who saw Hadassah as one of their own. As I said earlier, the fact that she was not American born had an effect beyond anything we'd expected. Wherever she went, people threw their arms around her; when she gave luncheon speeches, the new Americans on the kitchen staff would quietly emerge to listen to her. In early September, she visited the Lopez bakery in the Hispanic section of Milwaukee. José Lopez Sr. had started a bakery after leaving Mexico in 1967 with only $20 in his pocket. In recent years, he had expanded his operations and built two new bakeries. He'd handed over the original to one son, provided a second bakery for another son, and started a new one for his wife and himself. That was the one Hadassah visited, and when she entered the bakery, she was warmly surrounded by the people there.

She bought some Mexican pastries and passed them out to the press, who were all over her. Then she tied on an apron and went to work in the kitchen, learning to make a twisted Mexican bread. When she first went into the back, Mr. Lopez grasped her hands and held them. With tears in his eyes, he told her of his difficult journey from a poverty-stricken immigrant to where he stood that day, a proud and successful American citizen, with his own business and the wife of the vice presidential nominee visiting him.

Even if the expert campaign consultants had tried to weigh the separate impact of Hadassah's origins on the ticket, they couldn't have foreseen what a broad range of people she would touch. For a lot of first-generation Americans, she became a symbol of what was possible for them and their children in America. She looked right into people's eyes and talked straight into their hearts. I liked the way she described it. She said she was making "eye contact with America."

CHAPTER SEVEN

Back in 1989, after I was elected to the Senate, a union leader told me a story about a boy and his wagon to explain how he felt on election night. Now, this man's union had supported my opponent that year, Senator Lowell Weicker, the incumbent, who was expected to win easily. So his first meeting with me was awkward. Here's the story he told me.

A little boy is pulling his wagon along the sidewalk when the wheels fall off. "I'll be damned," he mutters, and he picks up the wheels and reconnects them to the wagon. He starts pulling the wagon along the sidewalk when again the wheels fall off. This time, growing more frustrated, the little boy shouts out loud, "I'll be damned."

Just then, the boy's minister comes by and says, "Son, I heard what you said, and I have to tell you that when something bad like that happens, you shouldn't swear. You should affirm your faith in God."

So the little boy puts the wheels back on the wagon and pulls it along the sidewalk, and wouldn't you know, the wheels fall off again. But this time, with his minister right there, instead of swearing, the boy dutifully shouts out, "Praise the Lord!"

And the wheels rise off the sidewalk and reattach themselves to the wagon—and the minister says, "I'll be damned."

"That's the way we here in Washington felt about your election," the union leader told me. "We all said, 'I'll be damned.'"

I told this story often throughout the fall of 2000, and each time I gleefully concluded, "That's the way I felt when Al Gore selected me to run for vice president. Miracles happen, so praise the Lord!"

I was thrilled to be chosen and excited about the opportunities ahead, but I wasn't eager to leave the job I had. I love serving in the Senate. There will come a time when I should move on, but that time had certainly not arrived in 2000. I had already declared I was running for reelection when Gore chose me. And I had been renominated unanimously by the Connecticut Democratic Party in July, so when I made it to the short list of vice presidential nominees, I began to mull over the possibility of running in both races.

I knew it had been done before. I knew that Lyndon Johnson had run for both in 1960, and that Lloyd Bentsen had also done so in 1988, when he ran with Mike Dukakis. But Johnson and Bentsen had been Texas senators, governed by Texas law. I didn't know if there was something in Connecticut law that would hold me back. A member of my staff made very quiet inquiries, and discovered, interestingly enough, that the last time this question arose was in 1964, when Chris Dodd's father, Senator Thomas Dodd, made it to President Johnson's short list for running mate. Ultimately Johnson chose Hubert Humphrey, but before he did, the Connecticut attorney general ruled there would be no legal impediment to Dodd's running for both offices at the same time, so precedent had been set.

By the time I was selected, I had decided. I would run—hard—for vice president, and I would also run for reelection to the Senate, unless, of course, I was asked to make a choice between the two as a condition of being nominated for VP. That would have been a difficult decision, but fortunately I was not asked to make it. I was very grateful to have been chosen and totally committed to doing everything I could to help Al win, so I would not have run for the Senate again if I'd felt it would hurt the ticket. But it didn't make sense to me that someone in California, Florida, or Pennsylvania would vote against our ticket because I was running for the Senate in Connecticut.

And the people of Connecticut, bless them, seemed not to be bothered by my decision. They were like my extended family, proud that I had been asked to run for VP but aware that I might not get elected. And Connecticut Democrats didn't want a fight over the nomination to replace me in the middle of the campaign. Under Connecticut rules, the selection of a successor would be made by the seventy-two-member state central committee; it would not be a public process.

My decision was more controversial among my Democratic colleagues in the Senate. At the time, there were forty-six Democrats and fifty-four Republicans in the Senate. Several key seats were in the balance that election season. If Al Gore and I were elected, and I resigned the Senate, Connecticut governor John Rowland, a Republican, would appoint my replacement, thereby handing another seat and perhaps continued control of the seat to the Republican Party. A few got so agitated about this possibility that they talked about circulating a letter asking me to step down from the Senate race. But it never got that far. "Look," said one of my friends in the Senate, "if you were where we are, you'd be asking that you not run for both offices. And if we were where you are, we'd be running for both offices."

The question never became a national campaign issue. It would bubble up in interviews now and then; I would answer the question and then quickly move on. The *Hartford Courant* ran editorials urging me to step down. So did *The New York Times.* But the voters in Connecticut reelected me to the Senate in November with 64 percent of the vote, while our presidential ticket was carrying the state with 58 percent. I am very grateful to my longtime friend Ken Dagliere, who managed my 2000 U.S. Senate campaign and to my Connecticut Senate office staff, led by Laura Cahill and Joan Jacobs, whose service to the people of Connecticut was clearly appreciated. Today I joke that in 2000, the majority of people in Connecticut voted for me twice—legally. But I know how much I owe the people of my state for supporting our national ticket and still giving me the honor of continuing to serve them in the U.S. Senate.

When *The New York Times* wrote about the announcement rally at the War Memorial in August, it commented on my "boyish delight at having been chosen as Mr. Gore's running mate and [my] obvious relish for the political combat ahead." Since I was fifty-eight years old when Al picked me, I was very pleased with that "boyish"; as for the "delight" and "relish," their reporter got it right there, too. I love to campaign, and I love a good political fight. I was about to experience both on a larger stage than ever before, so I was charged up.

I like campaigning because I like meeting people. In some ways, it is as simple as that. For that, I am probably indebted to the example of my parents, who, while not actively involved in politics, were always volunteering in their community and reaching out to meet people. I learned early on in my political career that the first thing you've got to decide, before you decide whether to run for some office, is why you are running. You've got to have a cause, you've got to believe in it, and you've got to be persistent. I remember watching Bill Clinton, who was running for president, stand in the rain in eastern Connecticut one day for almost ten minutes, trying to convince one very skeptical and outspoken young voter to support him.

Nobody is better with people on the campaign trail

than Clinton. But over the years, I've had the luck and privilege to closely observe many of the political greats as they campaigned—John F. Kennedy, of course, and Hubert Humphrey, the Happy Warrior. I have to admit I was a closet fan of Ronald Reagan's campaigning. His warm, strong, optimistic attitude greatly impressed and moved me. And there were my Connecticut heroes, among them, Abe Ribicoff, Tom Dodd, Ella Grasso.

From each of them I learned a lot about campaigning, lessons that over the years I had probably unconsciously incorporated into my own campaign style. In the end, though, you've got to do what is natural for you. If you don't, the voters will see right through your act and turn away from you.

For me, one of the great joys of the 2000 campaign was that the campaign style I had developed in Connecticut worked nationally. Of course, the rallies were bigger and more frequent than in my Connecticut campaigns, but I loved them. I also learned how much work goes into a national campaign.

In addition to the team that Nashville gave me to travel on our plane, the *Spirit,* I brought two people on board full-time from my Senate office: Nao Matsukata, one of my legislative assistants, became the point of policy contact between my Senate office and the campaign; and Melissa Winter, my executive assistant/scheduler, became the point of contact between the campaign and the rest of my world—family, staff, politicians, and so forth. Melissa and Dave O'Brien also helped move me personally around the

Night flight of the Spirit*. The candidate studies; the campaign manager, Tom Nides, yawns. Second row on the left: trip director David O'Brien asleep and personal assistant Melissa Winter. On the right: researcher Chris Ulrich and political director Tina Flournoy. Back row: communications director Kiki McLean, asleep, and researcher Nao Matsukata.*

country—making sure, for example, that I ate regularly and that my clothes were clean and pressed. From August to November, my life changed. I never saw the front door or lobby of a hotel; I always entered privately. I never was allowed to drive a car. In fact, on the Saturday in December when it was all over and the Secret Service departed, the first thing I did after sunset was take my family out for a drive.

In addition to the planeload of staff, another large group of people in Nashville was assigned to me and my campaign. They had a lot of detailed policy and logistical work to do and did it very well. Every campaign day involved an enormous amount of planning and implementation. After the Nashville brain trust put a state on my schedule, an advance team made largely of "twenty-somethings" was sent out, usually four to six days before the event. My admiration for these kids grew as the campaign progressed. Taking a break from school or jobs, they became itinerant workers, traveling from coast to coast and city to city, ahead of the candidates, sleeping little, working feverishly to find a rally site, work with local constituency groups to build a crowd, and then get the crowd whipped up before I arrived. It was no wonder I enjoyed myself when I got there.

But as the campaign went on, I began to wonder whether there were too many rallies. They were obviously important to build enthusiasm among our local supporters, but we needed something more than the candidate shouting to excited crowds to convey our message through the media to people who weren't there. So Nashville agreed to supplement the rallies with a great variety of settings in which I could talk seriously about our ideas and plans and hopes, but could also listen to people. We went to a town hall meeting in a Missouri school and roundtable discussions in an Ohio hospital, a Michigan union hall, a Milwaukee senior center, a Pittsburgh high-tech company, an Oregon elementary school, and many more places.

On Labor Day afternoon, I stopped at a great minor league ball park where thousands of building trades union members and their families were watching a Toledo Mud Hens (that's right) game. The folks were having a great time, and they gave me a boisterous welcome. As I worked the crowd, a gray-haired gentleman suddenly appeared and said that he wanted to give me a lucky Irish coin, a punt, and that if I carried it every day, we'd win the election. He said the last person he gave such a coin to was Bill Clinton in 1992. I carried the coin every day and I still have it. When the campaign ended, I asked our chairman, Bill Daley, who I assumed was an expert on lucky Irish coins, why it hadn't worked. "It did work," Daley answered. "You got more votes than the other ticket. The problem must have been that nobody told the Irish coin it also had to win the electoral college."

I was even able to bring to the national campaign my favorite Connecticut way to meet people—visiting diners. When I was first elected to the Senate, I found that the people who came to my office were mostly representatives of organized interest groups. They have a right to speak, and I have a responsibility to listen to them, but that's not enough. I wanted to reach out to the unorganized majority of people and find out what they were thinking. So I started to hold open town meetings but was disappointed that a lot of the people who showed up were also representatives of the special interest groups.

Someone suggested I try visiting diners, and I did, inviting the local media to come along with me. It's more than a decade later, and I have made more than 150 diner stops in Connecticut, going from table to table with coffee (we call this the "cup of Joe with Joe tour"), meeting the random sample of people there, and asking, "What's your name? What do you do? How's it going? Do you have any messages you would like me to bring back to Washington? How do you think the president's doing?" Over the years, I've learned a lot from these conversations. It's certainly not a scientific process, but my diner companions have given me more good ideas than public opinion polls have—and they cost much less.

I wondered whether this kind of quiet campaigning would work out across the big country, and the fact that it did says a lot about how much Americans share in the midst of their diversity. If you look at an electoral map of America, you clearly see regional differences, and when you look down from the air, you can't help but be struck by the glorious variety of the American landscape. But on the ground, in 2000, a lot of America looked the same to me.

First, what's been built on the land everywhere—McDonald's, Wal-Mart stores, and all the rest—brings a uniformity to so many of the roads we traveled. But, more powerful, as I met and listened to people at the diners and discussions, were the shared experiences, the common values, hopes, and fears, and the broadly held faith in God. Campaigning is physically and intellectually demanding, and it can be exhausting, but it is also a great human journey. In 2000, I sometimes thought of myself as Huck Finn, riding a raft along the Mississippi, approaching the next bend in the river, not knowing exactly what would be there, but excited and optimistic about what I would find. I was never disappointed. I learned a lot from the American people in the 2000 campaign, about how much our country is changing and yet how much its best values remain the same.

As we zigzagged across America, we saw countless examples of average people understanding that technology had changed the world and that they had to change with it, to be able to realize their dreams for themselves and their children. We saw the genius of technological innovation meeting up with the capital of gutsy entrepreneurship to form new businesses.

Did you know there are more high-tech workers in Orlando, Florida, than there are theme park employees? I learned that preparing a speech to give at a company called Cirent Semiconductor, Florida's largest manufacturer of integrated circuits, in Orlando.

Everywhere I went, I heard the stories behind the unprecedented prosperity of the 1990s. I saw how our government's fiscal responsibility, investments in education and research, and its support of trade had provided the groundwork for this economic success. And, most excitingly, as I traveled, I met the people who had made these changes happen—who planted the seeds and made our economy grow.

I stopped at a Visteon plant in Ypsilanti, Michigan, where they manufacture automobile parts. It's a spin-off from Ford. New business management theories are being put to the test at this plant, with brilliant results. With the negotiated cooperation of the United Auto Workers, the place has been reinvented, top to bottom, literally. The executives are no longer off in an imperial wing of their own. Their desks have moved closer to the work floor in offices they share with the foremen and labor leaders, while their old offices have been transformed into an exercise room for all employees. The workers elect their foremen to serve for a period of time, and the foremen can be reelected or not. Everywhere you look, the equipment is state-of-the-art high-tech. This is not your grandfather's auto parts factory.

I stopped to talk to one of the employees, a man who was working on a very sophisticated piece of machinery. He was a bit older than most of the others, which is to say roughly my age. He said he'd been working at the plant for thirty years. "How do you feel to be surrounded by all this high-tech equipment?" I asked him.

Like it, he said.

"You must have seen a lot of changes in your years here, haven't you?"

"I have," he replied, "but I'll tell you this: If we didn't change, I wouldn't have had a job today, because if we weren't changing, this company would take these jobs out of Michigan. Maybe out of the States altogether, but certainly out of Michigan."

◈ As you travel on the campaign trail, the opportunity to sit down and talk with people about their lives and work and dreams can completely change your thinking. Something like this happened one day when our son Ethan and I found ourselves at a roundtable discussion in Kansas City.

The event was for "young voters," aimed at inspiring their participation in the campaign. I remember Ethan's words at that time: "Many of these 'young' voters were indeed under twenty-six or so, but most were single mothers who were desperately trying to make ends meet. They were meaningless as a profile of 'youth' but meaningful as a slice of the American public that was still scraping things together even in the wake of unprecedented prosperity."

What was most humbling about this experience was how hard these women were working and how uncertain their futures would remain unless they had a few

breaks. All fit into that category called "the working poor." But Ethan and I both realized at that moment that this was a case where slogans and descriptions can be limiting or even just inaccurate. We needed to change the way we looked at these women. If we were to think of them as having the potential to grow into the middle class, we would all benefit. The middle class has always been critical to us as Americans. We need to make sure that we continue the programs that are needed to grow the middle class. These women just needed someone to jump-start their lives so they could become a part of the great growing middle class in this country.

⧈ Hadassah was right. Not only has America's strong middle class kept this country stable and free, its continuing growth is the best evidence that America truly is a land of opportunity. Becoming part of it was what had drawn so many generations of new Americans, including my grandparents, to come here. So what better purpose could government have than to help grow and, I would add, "protect" the middle class in the sense of making sure they are treated fairly as consumers, as workers, and, increasingly, as investors?

One very early morning, I was sitting with a bunch of firefighters eating breakfast in their Hollywood, Florida, firehouse, and I asked them what they usually talked about at breakfast.

The answer that came back was surprising. It wasn't anything I would have guessed—sports, family, firefighting, sex. The answer was, "On a normal morning at breakfast, we talk about the stock market."

That told me a lot about a remarkable change that has occurred in our economy over the last two decades. Capitalism has been democratized. That's one of the ways we are growing the middle class. The old, hard lines between owners and workers have been blurred. Millions of workers are also owners today.

The America I saw in the 2000 campaign was not an "us vs. them" country, or a "people vs. the powerful" economy, where when one group gains another must lose. It had much more the feel of President Kennedy's "A rising tide raises all boats," where we work together to increase the size of our economy, and most people do better as a result

---

In July, after I had made the short list for vice president, the Gore campaign asked my staff to help with a New York City fund-raiser at the home of singer Paul Simon. Sherry Brown, my longtime campaign manager and fund-raiser, was eager to show the Gore camp that we could flex some fund-raising muscles. Now, believe me, raising money in New York City on a Sunday night in July for *anybody* or any organization—no matter how noble the cause—is a challenging task. But Sherry felt strongly that if we did well at

An early breakfast with firefighters at the firehouse in Hollywood, Florida.

this, it would elevate my chances of being. "I think we're being auditioned," she told me, and she may have been right. Certainly, she did a terrific job, bringing in a group of loyal supporters from Connecticut and New York. The fund-raiser was a highly successful event, and when I got the VP nod, I asked Sherry Brown to be my chief fund-raiser for the campaign, with offices at the Democratic National Committee (DNC).

On that first day in Nashville, my senatorial staff and my newly appointed campaign team gathered at a meeting with the Gore staff. "We all took our places, listening to what our roles might be and what was expected of us," Sherry recalls. As the meeting took place, calls apparently began coming in to DNC headquarters from my supporters. "The phones were ringing off the hook," Sherry said, "and the people on the other end wanted to talk to a Lieberman person. I was dispatched to lead that effort."

In that capacity, one of the first calls she fielded was from a man whose name she doesn't remember. "I think he was from Colorado and worked at a dot-com. He had either met the senator once at some conference or he had heard him on some talk show. He just picked up the phone, called the DNC, and said he wanted to talk to a Lieberman person. Eventually his call made its way to my desk. He quizzed me about my history with Joe Lieberman. He wanted to make sure he was speaking with someone who could assure him that if he made a donation, it would, indeed, help the ticket. I gave him my standard rap: We needed hard dollars; the party gets the vote out, and runs ads in target states, and that yes, if he gave money to the DNC, it would be helpful to Joe Lieberman because it would be helpful to the Democratic Party. He thanked me politely, got my address, and I figured we'd probably get a $500 check from this nice young man.

"A few days later, I was opening mail while discussing staff issues with the many volunteers who showed up to help us get organized. When I became silent in midsentence, they became curious. I was holding a check to the Democratic National Committee for $40,000 from the man I had spoken to and his wife. It was the most in hard dollars that they could give as a couple. A simple 'Hope this helps! Good luck!' was on the card. I wish I remembered his name; I wish I could tell him how important he was to my confidence in pushing ahead, because at that moment, I knew we were on our way."

The outpouring of support for the DNC was fantastic. We broke fund-raising records wherever we went. At these events, I'd usually tell the following story about my folks.

My father owned what in Connecticut is still called a "package store," Hamilton Liquors on Hamilton Avenue in Stamford. He retired shortly after being held up for the third time, but until he did, every day, at the end of a long day, he would bring the proceeds home and spread them out on the kitchen table and count the money. And every night, my mother would come to his side and ask, "Henry, what kind of a day have we had?"

"Well," I'd tell those at the fund-raisers, "I want you to know that I'm going to call my mom tonight and tell her that we have had one great day here in Boston"—or Austin, or wherever we happened to be. The crowds roared, and it pleased me to bring out that story. It made me feel that my father, who didn't live long enough to see this wonderful chapter of my life, was somehow with me on the campaign trail. And he would have enjoyed the tale as much as my audiences did.

That reminds me, a funny thing happened in 2000. I became known for being funny. It began on opening day. At the announcement rally in Nashville on August 8, I told the crowd I was surprised that the Republicans' first reaction to my selection had been to say that "George Bush and I think alike." Well, I said, "with all due respect, I think that's like saying the veterinarian and the taxidermist are in the same business—because either way you get your dog back." That, of course, is a time-honored brand of political humor that I've always enjoyed using: take humorous jabs at the other party. "Two weeks ago [at their convention]," I told the Democratic National Convention in Los Angeles, "our Republican friends tried to walk and talk a lot like us. But let's be honest. We may be near Hollywood tonight, but not since Tom Hanks won an Oscar has there been that much acting in Philadelphia." That brought down the house, and it was a very big house.

In being newly regarded as humorous, I was undoubtedly benefiting from low expectations. When Al Gore asked me to be his running mate, most of the news reports said that I'd been selected for my "seriousness of purpose," even "rectitude." When a crowd is prepared for someone like that, you don't have to do much to make them laugh. From the start of my political career I must have been seen as somber, because I remember Joe Dinielli, a colleague in the Connecticut State Senate during the 1970s, inviting me to participate in a fund-raising roast for him in his Bristol district and saying, "It will be funny just watching you *try* to be funny." I can hardly imagine what Joe would have said then if I'd told him that in 1999 I'd actually be voted "the funniest celebrity in Washington." (Of course, when I proudly reported this to my daughter Rebecca, she said, "That's a sad commentary on Washington, Dad.")

The fact is, my sisters and I were raised to laugh at life's foibles, and while my father was a serious man, he would laugh heartily at a good joke. My mother and grandmother brought all the wry and resigned humor of European Jewry into our home as exemplified in the Yiddish line I often heard, *"Mensch tracht und Gott lacht,"* loosely translated, "People plan and God laughs," but always with the implicit message that no matter what we do, God will have the last laugh (as is, of course, appropriate). Our family vacations, such as they were, tended to be weekends at resorts in New York's Catskill Mountains, where, after brain-numbing amounts of food, we'd howl at the comedians. And the television of my youth in the 1950s was full of brilliant comedy—from Sid Caesar to Red Skelton, from Bud Abbott and Lou Costello to George Burns and Gracie

Allen. That humor seeped into my subconscious and made surprising appearances in the 2000 campaign.

One time I was campaigning with Hadassah and during her speech she made an adorable, silly mistake. Everyone laughed, and I found myself shouting, "Say good night to the people, Gracie." And Hadassah, not missing a beat, replied, "Good night to the people, Gracie."

I took to introducing my praise of how much the economy had improved under Clinton-Gore by doing an old Abbott and Costello routine. Abbott says, "Lou, if you had $50 in one pants pocket and $100 in the other, what would you have?" And Costello answers, "Somebody else's pants."

That, I would go on to say, was how a lot of people had felt eight years before.

Sometimes the jokes would take a more sophisticated turn. "Standing here today," I began a speech on the economy to a large audience at Southwest Missouri State University in Springfield, "I am reminded of the time President Kennedy was invited to give a speech on the economy at a college in upstate New York. He and the dean of the school were political adversaries. When Kennedy arrived, he asked the dean, 'Are you still trying to convince everybody that we Democrats are fools?'

"'No, Mr. President,' the dean replied. 'That's why we invited you here. So they could find out for themselves.'" *Ba-da-boom*. The Missourians *roared,* and were drawn more comfortably into my speech on the Gore-Lieberman economic plan.

I even got to cross careers and act like a real comedian in appearances on Jon Stewart's *Daily Show* and Conan O'Brien's late night show. I had a blast on both. For Jon I offered a series of special ethnically-oriented bumper stickers for our ticket:

GORE-LIEBERMAN—NO BULL, NO PORK

WITH MALICE TOWARD NONE AND A LITTLE GUILT FOR EVERYONE

And a special one for gun owners: LOX AND LOAD

Conan and I exchanged some quips, and then he gave me the opportunity of a career: to sing "My Way" on national television. Two weeks later, Tony Bennett sang at a fund-raiser for us at the Wild Horse Saloon in Nashville. When I met Tony, he said, "I heard you sing 'My Way' on Conan's show. You're good."

It doesn't get much better than that, folks.

Someone once asked me if there are spiritual roots to my humor, and what came to mind was one of my favorite lines from the Psalms: "This is the day which the Lord has made. Let us rejoice and be glad thereon."

I certainly told the "praise the Lord" story about the boy and the wagon a lot during the 2000 campaign, because it made the "Miracles happen" point. And when appearing in a house of worship, regardless of denomination, I loved sharing the story about the man who was blessed to speak with God:

In awe of the Lord's freedom from human constraints of time and space, he asks, "Lord, help me understand, what is a second of time like to you?"

And God answers, "A second, my son, to me is like a thousand years to you."

The man then asks, "Lord, help me understand in my own earthly way—what is a penny like to you?"

"To me," the Lord declares, "a penny is like a million dollars to you."

The man pauses and then asks, "Lord, will you give me a penny?"

"Yes," God answers. "In a second."

So, God *does* get the last laugh.

CHAPTER EIGHT

One night while I was campaigning in New Jersey, I had a dream about my father, and it made me want to visit his grave.

We were set to attend a fund-raiser that day and make a few other campaign stops, but I couldn't shake the feeling that I had to go visit his grave in Bergen County near Paramus, New Jersey. So everyone just completely changed the schedule around. Somehow the motorcade found its way to the cemetery. My staff stayed in the car, and the Secret Service watched me, but from a distance. They understood. It was a beautiful sunny early fall day, and they left me alone to visit my father.

Afterward, I took everyone to visit Goldie, whose American name is Rose Lazarus. Like my mother, Goldie was a graduate of Auschwitz, and her brother had been married to my mother's sister before they were both killed in the Holocaust. Goldie insisted we stop by her house in Paramus and have lunch. Her house is a three-level brick suburban home, filled to the brim with every kitchen gadget and with extra cots and linens always ready for anyone who might need to be taken in. Everything in Goldie's house is set up to "service" family and neighbors; it would be impossible to count the number of people who have been nursed back to health by her chicken soup.

"Ess, ess"—eat, eat. The survivor community has many women like Goldie who believe that there is never enough they can do or make for their children or friends, so it was no surprise when I walked in to find that Goldie had prepared platters of food. They were heaping with sandwiches stuffed with tuna fish; there were salads and pickles. And here I was, surrounded by the Secret Service team and a staff, gripping their binders, filled with schedules that never cease.

Goldie had hugs for everyone. I'm not sure the Secret Service were used to being hugged by strangers, and they certainly never join you for a meal when they are working. But Goldie just kept offering more and more food and drinks until finally the agents succumbed. We carried trays laden with sandwiches out to the cars surrounding Goldie's property.

It was during that same trip to New Jersey that I met with a group of Jewish community leaders, as well as several rabbis, at an attorney's office. It was the day before Rosh Hashanah, the Jewish New Year, and when I stood up to speak to them, I looked them in the eye and said, "I understand that you're sitting around this table now and thinking, What am I doing here the day before Rosh Hashanah when I have no time?"

And their faces lit up! They all started nodding their heads up and down, and I said, "But you know what? Think about it. Here's the first Jewish American candidate. Where else should you be at this moment?" They got up and started introducing themselves, saying, "Yes, yes, that's exactly what I was thinking, and yes, you're exactly right." And several went back and wrote sermons about Joe's candidacy. We have those sermons collected in a book by a friend, along with many others given during the High Holidays in 2000.

Traveling got a lot easier after I got the plane, but I can't say life did. My house was no longer run by me; some days it was almost unrecognizable to me. Some days *I* was unrecognizable. One day when someone behind a rope line in Iowa asked me how I felt, I said, "Forget a bad hair day. I'm having a bad *face* day!" Once, leaning back in a plane seat, soaking my fatigue-swollen eyes with chamomile teabags in a pathetic attempt to make the swelling go down, I whispered to a staffer, "When this is all over, Joe's going to owe me some plastic surgery." (FYI, I haven't collected yet.)

Even when you think you've figured out a way to maintain a separation between your private life and your public life, you haven't. We went to a dear friend's wedding—a most personal event—but people treated us as if we were at a political rally. "Hey, we're from Chicago!" "We're from Albuquerque!" People kept dropping by the table, and finally the bride's grandparents, who were at our table, said, "Does this happen to you often? Do you ever get to finish a meal?" Ah, well, what are you going to do? Stop going to the weddings of dear friends?

You literally sacrifice your private life and your personal time. Relationships require time; whether it is a friendship or a marriage, you need time with that person. Joe once said that everywhere he went on the campaign trail, members of the local painters union (the International Union of Painters and Allied Trades, to be exact) were there—everywhere. Their appearances at every campaign stop, regardless of how remote it might be, meant a lot to him. However, when it occurred to Joe that between August and November of 2000, he was seeing more of the painters than he was of me, he was not so happy.

Even if you're out there with your husband on the road, when he's the candidate he's always knee deep in people, so you rarely get to be alone.

You miss your dear friends, so you invite one or two to come on a trip with you. They can ride with you from point A to point B, but they can't ride with you from point B to point C because you've got media interviews then. Or staff time. This is not a good way to keep your friendships going.

The lines between your public life and your private life blur even in your *own* head. Listen, these campaigns can lead you to behave in very strange ways. You want to have an argument with your husband, you're going to have it in front of the Secret Service. You want to tell your husband you love him, chances are you're going to have to tell him in front of others, maybe hundreds, even thousands, of others.

One night in October, Joe and I met up at a fundraiser at a beautiful home in Philadelphia. I hadn't seen him in a few days, and even though we were in the same tent in our host's backyard, we were at separate tables. So we were *still* apart. When they asked me to introduce Joe, I suddenly heard myself saying over the microphone, "Look, I just want to say to Joey that I believe in you and I love you so much."

And when he got up, Joe said, "This is very weird, because we're talking to each other through all of you who are good enough to be here, but sweetheart, I love you, too."

That public private moment was much sweeter than another reunion we had in Miami. It was a Friday afternoon. We were going to spend Shabbat together, and we had been apart since the previous Shabbat. I had been taken to a "hold" in a schoolhouse, sitting on the telephone for six . . . seven . . . ten interviews. I was all prepared for that Shabbat evening. I had the candles; a lovely dinner was planned at the hotel where we were staying. But first we had a rally, and we all waited anxiously for Joe, who was flying in from somewhere. Members of my staff were talking on cell phones with members of his staff, and they kept giving me travel updates: "He's twenty minutes out, Hadassah" or "Just ten minutes more." I was so excited.

"You know what?" I suddenly asked. "Why don't I go out and meet him? Nobody ever does that—just wait outside like a normal person. I want to go out, and I want to be there when he pulls in."

I hurried outside of the schoolhouse to the corner to look out for the car. A big crowd had already gathered for the rally. We waited. And we waited. And finally I heard and saw his motorcade, and I waved my arms around. Come on, Joey, come on.

Then I saw him through the tinted windows of the car. He was on the phone. He wasn't looking for me, he was working. I just iced up. The car pulled up, and he kept talking. I couldn't open the door; there are rules about that. Only the Secret Service does that. I was dying. And he looked up and saw the frustration on my face, and he saw that I was ice, and he grew frustrated, too, because it wasn't his fault. He was actually talking to one of our kids. But there we were, surrounded by a crowd all ready to walk to a rally with us, and a hundred cameras were trained on us. Ready to record our reunion . . . and my frustration.

Joe knew he had to keep those cameras out of our private life, to keep them from seeing what was going on. So he climbed out of the car and said, "Sweetheart, kiss me and look to the left."

What a moment! We're about to kiss, and I'm being

told "You're on Candid Camera." My kiss, supposed to be so spontaneous, is now being filmed. I have to admit, though, that a few minutes later someone took a great picture of us at the rally, because what happened there is that Joe started to tease me like crazy. Like *crazy*! He started saying to the crowd, "Oh, I haven't seen Hadassah in so long, I can't wait to see her tonight." I was mortified! He was saying something bordering on the intimate to a crowd of a few thousand people!

Joe and I love being in love, and we have to be in touch with each other throughout the day. Most days, if he just has two seconds free, he'll pick up the phone and call me. Everyone he works with knows that's what he'll do. But during the campaign that was impossible, and the separation was awful. Joe grounds me; I trust him. I need Joey.

You would think that having been a political spouse since 1983, I'd have been prepared for the craziness of the campaign. I wasn't. It had taken me some time, but as I had experienced the ups and downs of being married to someone in public office, I had come to understand the pressures on a public servant. I will never forget the morning in 1988 after Joe won the Senate seat. It had been such a hard race, and now our lives were going to be turned around because we would have to move to Washington. I woke up thinking, We've won, now we can rest a bit. But instead, Joe was already up and getting dressed. I said, "Joey, where are you going?"

He looked at me as though I should have known the answer. "I'm going to thank the voters of Connecticut," he said.

"Oh, my God!" I had tears in my eyes. "What about *me,* Joey?" But he had to get up and thank the people for voting for him. Later that day, one of our friends who had helped him raise money urged him to fly to Washington the next day to start lobbying about the committees that he should be on. That, thank goodness, he did not do, regardless of the consequences.

◘ When the 1988 campaign was over, I was exhilarated but exhausted. After traveling the state, thanking people throughout Connecticut for the enormous opportunity they had just given me, Hadassah and I left for a vacation at Paradise Island in the Bahamas. I needed the time together alone and away as much as, probably more than, she did. The truth is that I am at least as dependent on her support as she is on mine. And that means that I don't like it when we are forced to be apart.

◈ Now I can joke about the separations that politics imposes on a couple. I can say politics is like an incurable blood disease. Some people have it worse than others, and some are blessed to find other people who can relate to them.

When I moved to Washington as the wife of a brand-new senator from Connecticut, I felt as if I had to start all over again. I will never forget when a dear friend of Joe's, Natalie Spingarn, a former press secretary in Senator Abe Ribicoff's office, held a "coming out" party upon our arrival. She had invited many of her colleagues from the media. I recall standing in her lovely Georgetown home, shaking hands and expressing gratitude to Natalie for her gracious open house. Of course, I kept repeating, Oh, Joe will be here soon—as soon as the Senate completes its last vote. I will never forget that evening, because it was my "maiden voyage" as a Senate spouse. You learn to wait and wait and wait. In the midst of all the handshaking, a reporter said to our hosts, "Well, Mrs. Lieberman will have to learn to understand Washington better. I guess she will have to learn to knit." This was in 1988. Matters have improved since then. Or, at least, *for the most part* improved.

In the early fall of 2000, a wonderful, funny friend joined me on the campaign trail for a few days and kept notes: "The next morning my understanding of being on the campaign trail began in earnest," Diane wrote. "H emerged wearing the blue pantsuit I had selected for her at Nordstrom's—and I was assigned to sit with her in the limo as we drove toward Lexington. . . . We arrived at the small restaurant in downtown Lexington where H had been assigned to pour coffee for the local patrons while they had breakfast. At the restaurant she also met up with the mayor and the press. I had to ask myself about the gender assignment of this duty, as to my knowledge, in all the diners J has visited, I don't recall him pouring the coffee for anyone."

◘ Now wait a minute, Diane. I make and *pour* the coffee in our house every morning.

◈ "After 'coffee,' H strolled down the main street in Lexington with the press covering her stroll. At the end of a few short blocks there was a park with big mesh horses as a symbol of Lexington's connection to the racing industry. H had her picture taken with a horse. That picture, along with her pouring coffee, ended up in the paper the next day.

"Next it was off on H's plane to Springfield, MO. . . . Our first stop in Springfield was a senior center, where H's job this time was to serve milk (do they ask J to serve milk?) (You got me that time, Diane. I've never poured milk except for our kids.) and then to take questions from the seniors, sit with them at a round table, and meet with the press. Next we were off to a major fund-raiser at a home located near a golf course in

Hadassah and campaign manager Sally Aman.

Springfield. Here I really felt for my friend. The very large kitchen was packed with people. H took the time to say hello and shake hands and have her picture taken with almost all of them—one at a time. Next, we were off to the very large living room, where there was to be more smiling, more handshaking and picture taking, and then some speech making. I positioned myself far away from H but in her direct line of sight and smiled a mischievous smile at her.... For a very brief millisecond, I got a heartfelt smile back. Next we were off to the airport. This time, I was forbidden from sitting in the car with her."

Life can get fairly lonely for a public servant's wife. In one state during the campaign, I rode to a political event with the governor's wife, who was a tremendous asset to her husband. As I reached the podium where I was scheduled to speak I looked around and asked the governor, Where's your wife? And he said, Well, why? Do you want her? And I said yes. If you don't object, yes, I'd like her up here with me.

It is said that in politics there are no permanent friends and no permanent enemies. Because of that, too few people confide in one another. And that includes spouses.

Once, I attended a discussion group on political spouses at a Democratic National Committee meeting. A woman stood to complain about how she had walked into some function and someone was shaking her husband's hand, a photographer or a journalist, and then she came along, and the person shook her hand—while never taking his eyes off her husband. She felt invisible.

I knew what she was talking about, and it made me so angry that I thought, Ugh, I can't stand it, and I made up a story on the spot. I said, That happened to me once. But you know what you can do that works in those situations? You grow the nail of your little finger, and the next time you shake hands with someone like that, you just stick the nail real hard into his palm. He'll look at you.

The other spouses stared at me when I told that story. They couldn't believe it, and, okay, they were right not to. But the point is that if you're married to a public official, you must learn to protect yourself. Sometimes the world sees you only as a symbol or an adjunct. It's hard, but you have to learn to protect your private self.

The Secret Service agents understood this. Ron Weiss, one of the heads of my detail, said to me, "You know, anytime you want to stop, we'll stop. You've got to do that sometimes, so you just tell us when you feel that way."

A few days later we were in Maine, and I was in the backseat of the car, looking out the window, and it was beautiful—the boats in the harbor, the ocean off in the distance—and I suddenly had this powerful feeling: I've got to get out of this car and see the water and breathe the Maine air.

I told the Secret Service agent and he signaled to everybody, We're stopping. We pulled over on the side of a hill, and there I climbed a dozen steps to a platform that overlooked the bay. The agent said to my staff and to the reporters following us, "Give her room, give her space, stay away." For two minutes, alone, I watched the water and listened to the sounds of the sea. It filled my heart. And got me ready to return to the campaign trail.

CHAPTER NINE

During 2000, someone told me that in the heat of a national campaign there are only two moods among campaign workers:

1. We're going to lose.
2. What job do I want in the administration?

In September 2000, the résumés were being polished. The Bush campaign had stumbled in the wake of our success at the convention. Bush's double-digit lead had evaporated after the Democratic National Convention, and even his negatives had risen above Gore's—39 percent vs. 29 percent for Al, according to one poll. "We let [Gore] come back to life," griped one Republican strategist. "It was a great blunder."

Not only was Bush having trouble getting back on his feet, Gore was indefatigable (and so, may I add, was I). We campaigned for twenty-four hours straight over Labor Day—from Philadelphia to Flint, to Tampa, to Toledo, to

Detroit. Bush, on the other hand, seemed to be working half as hard. Every time we turned around he was heading back to his Texas ranch for another weekend of R&R. A senior Gore staffer joked that while Al traveled with a "football," the briefcase containing the codes for a nuclear launch, Bush's aides also carried a "football" for their boss—it contained Bush's pillow.

Bush seemed testy and insecure. He kept mangling words. A microphone was left open and he was overheard describing Adam Clymer of *The New York Times* to Dick Cheney as "a major league asshole," to which Cheney responded, "Oh yeah, big time." And he got bogged down in a debate over presidential debates. When Bush complained to reporters, "Debates suck the air out of the campaign," it made him look as if he were trying to duck being compared to Al Gore, who was known to be a great debater.

Somewhere around the third week of September, Bush snapped awake. Some observers gave Laura Bush credit for shaking her husband and his campaign out of its stupor. I don't know if that's the case or not. I do know that the Republicans launched a strong counterattack.

Up until that point, Bush's campaign was mostly directed against Bill Clinton, promising to "restore honor and dignity" to the White House. But Al Gore had stood before the convention and declared, "We're entering a new time. We're electing a new president. And I stand here tonight as my own man." Now Bush had to broaden his attack and go more directly after Gore. The Republicans didn't stop their anti-Clinton rhetoric. They just added a series of new attacks that were intended to tarnish Al's appeal and credibility, and mine.

At a speech in Green Bay, Wisconsin, on September 28, Bush declared, "The vice president was seated right behind Bill Clinton at the State of the Union when the president declared, 'The era of big government is over.' Apparently, the message never took. . . . He offers a big federal spending program to nearly every single voting bloc in America. He expands entitlements without reforms to sustain them."

This was Bush's new refrain: Beware! Al Gore is a big government liberal in the guise of a New Democrat.

He was wrong. Gore's record was full of fiscal responsibility and government efficiency, but Bush *had* found a vulnerability nonetheless in the Gore campaign, whose strategy was to beat Bush on individual issues—prescription drugs, Social Security, Medicare, HMO reform. To turn the spotlight on Bush's vulnerability—lack of specificity and weakness with facts—our campaign made a lot of detailed proposals which allowed Bush to paint Gore as a candidate who had a government answer to every problem.

That's not all the Republicans did to Al Gore in September.

During a stump speech on prescription drug prices in Tallahassee, Florida, on August 28, Al said that Lodine, the arthritis medicine used by Tipper's mother, was the same medicine used to treat the Gores' dog, Shiloh, and that the drug was three times more expensive to buy for his mother-in-law than for his dog.

Three weeks later, *The Boston Globe* published an article pointing out inaccuracies in Al's statement, but also concluding that "Gore's overall message was accurate—that many brand-name drugs are much more expensive for people than for pets." The Republicans immediately flooded reporters with faxes of the *Globe* article and e-mails questioning Al's credibility. The media ate it up.

Introducing her husband, Dick Cheney, at rallies during the following days, Lynne Cheney told the cheering crowds, "I once wrote a book called *Telling the Truth,* and I am sending an autographed copy to the vice president." The Bush campaign hired a college student to climb into a dog suit, hung a sign around his neck that read "Lodine the Canine," and sent him to Gore events.

At the same time, after a very smooth and positive entry into the race, I began to come in for my share of political flak. The Bush campaign was circulating misleading information to the media that I had changed my position on Social Security, privatization, and affirmative action. I had not. The Anti-Defamation League's Abe Foxman intensified his criticism of my expressions of faith, complaining that I was "hawking religion." Then I appeared on an African American radio network and was asked whether I would meet with Louis Farrakhan, which a few leaders in the African American community whom I greatly respected had urged me to do. They said his bout with prostate cancer had changed him, and I should seize this moment to reach out to him. I said that although I had been deeply offended by Farrakhan's racist and anti-Semitic statements in the past, I was open to meeting with him on the chance that he might have changed. That brought another wave of criticism from the Republicans, the ADL, and some newspaper columnists.

Next, Bill Bennett, my comrade-in-arms in the culture wars, accused me of going soft on Hollywood after a Beverly Hills fund-raiser where I had said I would never support censorship of Hollywood but would continue to "nudzh" them to produce better entertainment with less violence and less sex. Bennett criticized my use of the Yiddish verb "nudzh" as too gentle. My response was that, based on long experience being "nudzhed"—particularly by members of my family—I would define the verb as "persistent criticism until one changes one's behavior." That seemed exactly like what he and I had been doing to the entertainment industry. In any case, I did not benefit from the exchange.

Within our campaign, all this caused an outbreak of anxiety at the end of September as we began to slip in the polls. But that dissipated when Bush was badgered into accepting the challenge to debate Gore—in fact, to debate him three times. Great, we thought, we'll win those straying voters back when we get to the debates in October. Al is an excellent debater, and there is no way the governor of Texas can gain comparable confidence with the facts a president faces in such a short time. As for me, I'd had my share of campaign debates, and I'd learned a lot from them. In 1988, my debate performances had been crucial to my narrow win over Senator Weicker. I had proved I could get in the ring with the pro and not only hold my own, but land some punches. That, to our surprise, was what Bush ended up doing to Gore in 2000.

The one vice presidential debate would be held on October 5 at the Norton Center for the Arts at Centre College, a small liberal arts school in Danville, Kentucky. Although the stakes were higher in the three presidential debates, I naturally wanted to do as well as I possibly could to help the ticket.

If it takes a village to raise a child, it apparently takes an army to prepare a vice presidential debater, or so I learned in 2000. Jonathan Sallet was our general. He'd worked on Al Gore's debate training teams in 1992 and 1996. ("I hold the American political record for the most days lodged in a vice presidential debate camp," says Jonathan.) Sheryl Wilkerson, a Washington attorney, left the FCC early in September to work with Jon, heading up a team that did debate research, and put together an issues book for me. It was big. It not only contained the basic papers on the widest range of issues, but it also included every position I had ever taken on any issue and the Gore campaign's position on all the issues.

It wasn't enough to simply be on track with the Gore

campaign. I needed to be able to defend and advance each and every position the campaign espoused, and to do so in a short, crisp, affirmative way.

The preparation was more extensive than anything I had ever experienced. But remember, the debate would be the third and final big moment of opportunity for me to make a real difference in the campaign.

Beginning in September—even before we knew whether the debates would occur and, if so, where and when—we crammed tutorial sessions into those rare times on planes or in hotel rooms when I had a few hours free. So I carried my briefing book everywhere. Jonathan seized chunks of time in the strangest places, suddenly appearing at a hotel where we were staying in Miami, just as the sun set on Saturday, for three evening hours of debate prep. Another time he worked his way into the schedule on a Friday afternoon in Chicago for two hours before the sun set. That time he brought a mock opponent and we had a practice debate.

Meanwhile, we worked together to strategize and analyze my opponent's vulnerabilities. Should I take on Cheney or focus my attacks on Bush? We studied tapes of Cheney's television appearances and analyzed ones from my Senate campaigns. I was surprised at how aggressive I'd been in my 1988 debates in the Senate race with Senator Lowell Weicker. A campaign strategist—probably

Carter Eskew, maybe the late Bob Squier—said to me back then, You know, you've got to convince the voters of Connecticut to fire Weicker and hire you. I'd clearly taken their advice to heart—and it had worked.

I am not by nature a combative person, but I can definitely be a fighter when I have something to fight for. In this case, I was ready to get aggressive again in the debate with Cheney, because the differences between his record and mine and Al's were so stark. But surprisingly, the pollsters and consultants counseled otherwise. Their survey and focus group results were clear. The public doesn't want another antagonistic debate. They're tired of nastiness; they crave a civil face-off. Good enough, I said to them, I wasn't planning to be mean-spirited or personally abusive, but I assume I should call attention to Cheney's far right record when he was in Congress; you'll want me to tell people he voted against Head Start? Against a free Nelson Mandela resolution? No, they said. The public feels that all happened too long ago. Even if we believe it's relevant to what kind of vice president he'd be? No, the pollsters said, if you throw old votes at him, the public will react negatively. (I was amused remembering how Lowell Weicker had responded to my closing the lead he had on me with a few weeks left in the campaign: he attacked votes I had cast *seventeen* years before. It almost worked.)

Along the way, we watched and analyzed good televised debates (bad ones, too) in national campaigns. It helped. Gore versus Quayle in 1992. I was told how upset President Clinton had been with Al because he felt Al had failed to stand up sufficiently for him against Quayle's attacks in that debate. That was worth remembering. Gore versus Kemp. There, Gore tended to repeat catchphrases a bit often, we noticed, but he was nevertheless very disciplined, very effective. We watched Bentsen turn that wonderful line on Quayle, "Senator, I served with Jack Kennedy. I knew Jack Kennedy, Jack Kennedy was a friend of mine. Senator, you're no Jack Kennedy." And in pained silence we watched a tape from 1988, when Mike Dukakis, who opposed capital punishment, gave a wooden, canned response to CNN's Bernard Shaw's provocative and direct question: If someone raped and killed your wife, would you change your position and advocate the death penalty for her attacker? Shaw was scheduled to moderate the debate between me and Dick Cheney. God only knew what he was cooking up for us.

On Sunday evening, October 1, with four days to go before the debate, I left the campaign trail for final, intensive debate training. Danville, Kentucky, is a lovely little town in the beautiful bluegrass country, ninety minutes south of Lexington. The campaign rented an old mansion owned by Eastern Kentucky University in the isolated hills of the nearby town of Richmond. Jon called this our debate camp, but because I'm a boxing fan, I said it felt like a boxer's training camp. So someone quickly made up a T-shirt for me that said "Fighting Joe Lieberman" on the front and "The Champ" on the back. They even found a book called *When Boxing Was a Jewish Sport,* by Allen Bodner, with tales of Benny Leonard, Barney Ross, "Battling" Levinsky, and "Slapsie" Maxie Rosenbloom—all of whom boxed before my time. My boxing heroes were Joe Louis, Rocky Marciano, Sugar Ray Robinson, and, of course, Muhammad Ali.

◈ **They secretly tried to get Muhammad Ali to be there when Joe arrived in Kentucky, because that's where Ali's from. He was willing, but he was returning from the Olympics in Sydney, Australia, and there was no way to make it happen in time. It would have really thrilled Joe; he's such a fan of Ali's.**

◘ I was tired. The fatigue I had suppressed on the campaign trail over the preceding weeks pushed its way out when I stopped to prepare for the debate in Kentucky and I had a lot of work to jam into just a few days. There was quite a large crowd of people—probably too many—in the house, available for research or any other need that might arise, but Sallet limited who could have contact with me. He didn't want, and I certainly didn't want, fifteen people making suggestions simultaneously. Camp rules were strict. Practice sessions were tightly organized, with a premium on giving me time to prepare by myself. Even Hadassah knew it would be better if she went off campaigning elsewhere in the daytime and returned at night.

◈ **Matt was there all week, and he was worried about Joe, although he didn't let on. But he told me he took a look at Joe and thought, Oh, my God. Where is he? What have they done with my father? Matt had never seen Joe so worn out. He said, "The light had gone out of his eyes. His brain was all there—but his soul wasn't coming through."**

Matt wondered whether "the preparation had reached the point of diminishing returns. Dad is a very disciplined, very hard worker, and the preparation was feeding that part of him. And certainly there's a lot you can prepare, and there's a lot worth preparing and brushing up on. But was all this necessary?"

◘ I was tired, and during some of the practice sessions I was tight, and I knew it. But when it was over, I was more prepared for this debate than I had ever been for anything like it in my life. And I was very clear about what I wanted to accomplish. Our goals were straightforward:

Remind voters of all the progress and prosperity of the last eight years, which our ticket was obviously best able to continue. Make clear the difference between Bush-Cheney and us on how we would use the new federal surplus responsibly to cut middle-class taxes, make investments in education and health care, and pay off the national debt.

Remind voters of our ticket's commitment to traditional moral values; reemphasize my roots, my faith, my values and Al's. Some of the characteristics that had led Al to select me as his running mate were getting lost in the campaign crossfire. We needed to reestablish that these values were at the heart of everything he and I planned to do.

Defang Cheney in what would presumably be his attack mode; and deflect and defend against all attempts to criticize Gore personally or to separate us as a team.

A few weeks before the debate, Al had said to me, "You know what Cheney's going to do during the debate, don't you?"

"What?" I asked.

"He's going to attack me. I hope you're ready."

Being a bit devilish, I said, "You mean at this big moment of my public life in a vice presidential debate, I've got to spend all my time defending *you*?"

Al was quiet for a second or two—and then he laughed heartily.

Al Gore had pretty much set a new standard for debate preparation in 1992 and 1996. At his debate camp they'd constructed a set that replicated the actual setting for the debate, down to the placement of the cameras. I was reluctant to go that far. Still, Sallet and company determined the measurement of the half-moon table at which we'd sit with CNN's Bernard Shaw, and they copied the chairs we'd be sitting in, so it would feel as familiar as possible when I walked out on that stage.

Monday night before the real debate on Thursday, we held the first of our practice debates. Jonathan kept the crowd small. Bob Barnett, my friend and lawyer, happens to be the Cal Ripken of political debate. His first mock vice presidential debate was in 1976, when he was part of the team that prepped Fritz Mondale for his debate with Bob Dole. Barnett worked with Mondale again in 1980, and in 1984 he ran the training for Geraldine Ferraro's debate with George Herbert Walker Bush. In 1988 he was a member of the team training Dukakis against Bush, again, and in 1992 he played Bush in at least twenty prep debates with Bill Clinton. In 1996, Barnett's wife, CBS correspondent Rita Braver, was covering the White House, so Bob had to recuse himself. But in 2000 he was back in a big way: as a member of Hillary Rodham Clinton's team, he played her opponent, Representative Rick Lazio, and in my camp he was Dick Cheney.

In that first practice, my ego took an early beating. Barnett's Cheney was brilliant—and shockingly well-informed. No matter what question the moderator threw at him, he nailed it. I had a moment of panic, then I looked across the mock debate table and realized that, of course, they had given Bob the questions! And he had his five-inch-thick briefing book in front of him. In it was everything Cheney had ever said, voted on, or done, all of it broken down into fifty-three categories. That Cheney would be aggressive and conservative seemed a given, so in each practice Bob played him with "varying degrees of negativity," as Stan Greenberg put it. Together we practiced every conceivable format and answered every question our team could think up.

On Tuesday, October 3, we had our daily practice debate early in the evening, then headed downstairs to the rathskeller of the old Kentucky mansion, where we watched the first debate between Al Gore and George W. Bush. I totally misread the debate. Because I was focused on the substance of the arguments—not whether or not Al sighed or whether he came off as condescending—I thought he did really well. He clearly was better prepared, had a better grasp of the facts, and in contrast, Bush looked inadequate to me. And that more or less was what I told reporters as the campaign kept me up until 2:00 A.M. doing postdebate analysis for a few networks and many local television stations across the country.

What I failed to appreciate was that the commentators had so lowered the bar for Bush that as long as he didn't make a major mistake, they would regard his performance as an accomplishment. Nor did I understand why Gore's mannerisms would become such an issue. And none of us were prepared for how aggressively the Bush people would attack Gore after the debate for even the slightest stray comments. "People have taken some misstatements and turned them into something mythic," a senior Gore adviser remarked afterward.

Gore would have two more chances; his next debates were scheduled for October 17 and October 27. But before that, I was up. The Gore campaign sent a small cavalry of its top consultants to Kentucky for last minute coaching. So, as Stan Greenberg put it, "early early *early*" the morning after the first Gore-Bush debate, an exhausted Greenberg, Eskew, Shrum, and Tad Devine boarded a plane for Kentucky. In retrospect, most would regret it. The Bush camp had been quick to attack Gore in its postdebate spin, and the next day it started running a sarcastic TV ad called "Trust," in which Bush was presented as a man who keeps his word, while Al was run down as a man who does not. It would have been wiser to keep the team in Nashville to coordinate the counterattack.

They did get to attend my best and last practice. I was more comfortable and confident. In response to an early question, I managed to work in a joke someone had prepared about the Gores' poor arthritic dog, Shiloh. Of Barnett's "Cheney"—after he attacked Gore—I said, "He's not only an attack dog, he actually attacked a dog." Jonathan had packed the house so I could get used to a live audience, and the room rocked with laughter. I never got to use the joke in the real debate. In retrospect, I think that was fortunate. It doesn't seem so funny now.

I felt good; I felt ready. But I badly needed a solid night's sleep, and the campaign had asked Hadassah to appear on a few network television shows the next morning. She'd have to get up at 5:30 A.M. It was unthinkable that we would sleep in separate bedrooms, but how could she get up without waking me so early on my big day? The solution: Heather Picazio would tiptoe into our bedroom and squeeze Hadassah's big toe until she got up—all very quietly. Heather worried all night she would accidentally squeeze my toe. Fortunately for all of us, she didn't.

It's the evening of the debate and we're in the hold behind the stage at Newlin Hall in the Norton Center for the Arts at Centre College in Danville. There's been little to do all day except wrap up loose ends and stay alert. Earlier, Michael Sheehan, a speech coach who had given me some helpful pointers in Los Angeles, arrived and offered last minute advice. Brighten up and grin more broadly, he said, because the camera takes away about a quarter of your smile and you can look sour even when you don't mean to. Gore's national security adviser, Leon

Fuerth, carefully fed me the name of the incoming president of Yugoslavia—Vojislav Kostunica (Kos-tu'-ni-cha). I practiced it until it rolled off my tongue. In Belgrade, reformers were storming the ramparts, and Slobodan Milošević would be driven out in a matter of days. George W. Bush had badly bobbled a Serbia question in his first debate with Gore. There was no way a question on Yugoslavia would fail to be asked tonight.

The kids are all here backstage, as is my mother, my sisters, Hadassah's brother, and their spouses. "Let's sing something," I say, and Matt, with his big, rich voice, starts in:

This little light of mine, I'm going to let it shine.
This little light of mine, I'm going to let it shine. . . .

We all dive in, *"Let it shine! Let it shine! Let it shiiiiiine!"* Our staff is used to such spontaneous outbursts from the singing Liebermans—the Von Trapps of American politics, as Becca says. Becca later told me she thinks Matt picked the song on purpose to subliminally remind me to "turn the light back on" in my eyes, the light he feared had been dimmed with exhaustion. Matt doesn't remember why he picked the song; it just came to him. And what a joyous, uplifting spiritual it is. If I wasn't pumped for the debate before, I am now!

The instant I walked out onto the stage and sat down, whatever anxiety I had floated away. Why? Probably because the expectation was over. I had entered the ring and knew I had trained hard and was ready. And I knew what I wanted to do.

I had worked hard that week to prepare an opening statement that would set a tone for the debate. After thanking our hosts and my family, I said, "My eighty-five-year-old mom gave me some good advice about the debate earlier today. She said, 'Sweetheart,' as she is prone to call me, 'remember, be positive and know that I will love you no matter what your opponent says about you.' Mom, as always, that was both reassuring and wise. I am going to be positive tonight. I'm not going to indulge in negative personal attacks. I'm going to talk about the issues that I know matter to the people of this country: education, health care, retirement security, and moral values. I'm going to describe the plan that Al Gore and I have for keeping America's prosperity going and making sure that it benefits more of America's families, particularly the hard-working middle-class families who have not yet fully benefited from the good times we've had. And Bernie, I'm going to explain tonight how we're going to do all this and remain fiscally responsible."

It was Dick Cheney's turn, and he surprised me, because one of the first things out of his mouth was, "And I, too, want to avoid any personal attacks." Where the presidential debate two days before had been acrimonious and noticeably tense, Cheney and I had both decided to strike a more civil tone. My opponent had shelved his dour and sometimes sour demeanor; he was reasonable in manner, conversational, even modestly comic. *Newsweek* later reported that on the morning of the debate, the Bush campaign pollster Matthew Dowd had briefed the Bush team and had urged Cheney to back off on any attacks at the debate. But what about Gore's "credibility"? Cheney had asked. "Couldn't I bring it up?"

"I wouldn't go personal," Dowd had replied. In other words, the Republican pollsters had found the same public mood that our pollsters had, which encouraged Cheney and me to have a good, substantive, civilized debate.

Toward the end, Bernie Shaw raised a pointed question that touched on the charges Republicans had leveled against me. He asked Cheney: "Have you noticed a contradiction or hypocritical shift by your opponent on positions and issues since he was nominated?"

To this, Cheney almost pleaded, "Boy, we've been trying to keep this on a high plane, Bernie."

So there were no fireworks. Every once in a while, there was a snappy comeback. When you are preparing for a national debate, your staff puts together a notebook of one-liners. I know Gore had one, as did Bush and Cheney. I had one, but most of the lines felt inappropriate to this debate, and the one time I used one, Cheney came back with a funnier line.

So for the most part we engaged in a thoughtful exchange of ideas. We tackled the surplus, tax cuts, education, inequality in women's pay, abortion, the former

Yugoslavia, when to deploy troops in the Middle East, Iraq, energy strategy, oil exploration in the Arctic National Wildlife Refuge, Social Security, gay rights, and more in a very substantive hour and a half.

Cheney and I disagreed on most issues, but we managed to disagree without being disagreeable.

◈ **And every now and then, they surprised everyone—by agreeing! When Bernie Shaw asked them about gay marriage, their answers weren't canned rhetoric programmed to please one interest group or another. What the voters saw were two men, from traditional backgrounds, who were trying to come to terms, in an open and tolerant fashion, with a controversial question in a changing world.**

◘ I was surprised when Bernie Shaw declared the debate over. The hour and a half had passed so quickly. And I was ecstatic. I had made the points I wanted to make on every question; I knew we'd had an interesting exchange; I thought we'd both done well. Tad Devine and Stan Greenberg told me later that night that they sat with a checklist of goals, points they hoped I would make, and I made them all.

◈ **What I have to say may sound like the words of a wife, but, really, they're the words of an observer. What is interesting about Joe is that he has a way of making people look good and feel comfortable. He brings out the best in people. Sitting there, I looked over at Matt and I could see him start to tear up a little because, as he said when it was over, "My dad was back. He'd been gone during the debate training, but he was back to-night and he was wonderful and it was a relief."**

◘ Al and Tipper called, and they were cheering with ex-citement. Al said, "You did just great; you did everything I could have wanted. I couldn't have been prouder of you."

We were flying high. We left the auditorium for a hot, screaming, exultant headquarters rally sponsored by the Kentucky Democratic Party and then went to a quieter but equally upbeat reception for some of my biggest support-ers who had flown in from around the country.

◈ **The response from the press and the public was out-standing. *The Washington Post* called the debate "seri-ous, well-informed, substantive, grown-up" and added, "Maybe the presidential tickets are upside down. The**

country might face a less troubling choice if Dick Cheney and Joseph Lieberman were the presidential candidates. . . ."

What you need to realize is this: Because he was a two-term senator, much was expected of Joe—and he totally lived up to everyone's expectations. As for Dick Cheney, he was someone who had been out of government for a long time and was widely seen as a hard-nosed conservative. This thoughtful Cheney surpassed expectations, so he gained a lot from the debate, too.

◘ It goes without saying that there were commentators who managed to find fault. Veteran columnist Mary McGrory complained that I had overdone my loyalty to Gore. "Lieberman was . . . lost in the mists of sycophancy . . . ," she wrote. "He was not the free spirit hailed by the media. He was a composite called 'Al-Gore-and-I.' "

But most of the pundits and editorial writers praised Cheney and me for the open, respectful exchange of ideas and opinions. "What viewers did see was both the seriousness and the dry wit that define both men, " said *The New York Times.* We proved that political debates don't have to be all attacks or all sound bites; we treated the voters with respect by respecting the importance of the issues. I'm tremendously proud of the debate. I felt, and will always feel, that we made a real and lasting contribution that night.

The next day, on a campaign plane, reporters asked Cheney about what a *Washington Post* reporter called "an increasingly direct assault on Gore's truthfulness by some of Cheney's surrogates, including his wife." Cheney snarled back, ripping into Al's "credibility problem" and going one step further. The U.S. military, Cheney charged, "is clearly worse off today than it was eight years ago." (It was an assertion that I recalled proudly a year later when that same military won a stunning victory against terrorism in Afghanistan.)

And me? After a postdebate "victory" lap around the increasingly critical state of Florida, and a wonderful family Sabbath in Washington, our campaign announced on Sunday that I would soon be leaving for a "Failed Leadership Tour" of Texas. My mission: To call attention to the serious wrongs George W. Bush had done to Texas as governor.

In other words, that one brief, shining moment known as "Danville" was over. The last month of the campaign had begun, and Dick Cheney and I were back on the vice presidential attack trail.

CHAPTER TEN

GORE OFFENSIVE TARGETS BUSH RECORD IN TEXAS

Lieberman to Lead Final-Month Assault

LONGBOAT KEY, FLA. —Vice President Gore launched a two-pronged, final-month attack on George W. Bush today that will use ads, Web sites and bus tours to lambaste Bush's record in Texas and lampoon what Gore's campaign calls the governor's "bumbling babblings." Gore himself plans to stick to his own issues and follow tradition in presidential races by dispatching his running mate, Connecticut Sen. Joseph I. Lieberman, as the attacker in chief. . . . In a separate offensive, the Democratic National Committee plans to publicize Bush misstatements by creating a gaffe Web site and issuing daily updates on "Bush bloopers"—statements that Gore aides consider tangled, inaccurate or simply funny. As a first strike, Democrats plan to post a Web video Monday of the governor struggling to explain his tax cut before a Florida audience this weekend. . . .

> Today, the Gore campaign issues a news release with the headline "Get It Right, Governor," which purported to document "Bush's latest policy bumblings."
>
> —Mike Allen, *The Washington Post,* October 9, 2000

The October "Failed Leadership Tour" was not my first visit to Texas to criticize Governor Bush's record there. The first was in September and was particularly memorable. It was a few days after Labor Day, and we were in Houston to call attention to Bush's dismal record on children's health care. It would be the first time we'd go after the governor on his own territory. It was late; we were hungry. The staff settled into one hotel room to eat, and I stepped into my bedroom to change into informal clothes and study the speech draft Paul Orzulak had just handed me for tomorrow. I got a few paragraphs in and said to myself, "I'll be damned if I'm going to make *this* speech."

It attacked Bush personally. It lacked substance. It wasn't me and it wasn't my voice. I remembered that President Clinton had wisely advised me always to say that our opponents were good men, but they had some very bad ideas for our country. One of the phrases I learned in the 2000 campaign was, "We have to push back." In other words, no, I don't like that schedule or this policy, and no, I won't do it or say it. It was time for me to push back.

I stepped out of my bedroom into the living room, where my staff was chatting. "I'm not going to make this speech," I said. "Paul"—I turned to my stunned speechwriter—"you've been with me for four weeks now. How could you think I would ever say these things? There's enough bad in Bush's record on children's health without me having to slash and burn him personally as if I'm some kind of mad dog. You need to go back at it and tell whoever in Nashville told you to write this that I am not going to give it."

I'd made it clear from the start of the campaign that I would go anywhere and do whatever the Nashville campaign team wanted me to do. That meant flying into two or three or four states a day, deplaning at 1:00 A.M. and being back up and alert at some location by 7:00 A.M., with a speech in my hand. Where did that speech come from? A day or two before, Paul would have called in to Nashville and spoken to our communications director, Jody Sakol, who would probaby have spoken to the campaign consultants. Jody would tell Paul the message of the day (economic growth, education, prescription drugs . . .), provide him with a focus, and inform him if there were specific points I should make. Paul would then draft remarks on his laptop on the plane, or in his room in the middle of the night, and give them to me for review and revision. But this time, Nashville and Paul were asking me to be someone I wasn't and someone I didn't want to be.

"Paul," I said, "when things come down from Nashville like this, you need to fight for me, because I'm not going to say things that aren't me."

And for the rest of the campaign he did.

The speech Paul rewrote that night stayed tough, but it

kept its focus on the facts—on Governor Bush's record and its impact on the citizens of Texas—and believe me, there was plenty to talk about without getting personal. Texas ranked forty-ninth out of fifty states in providing health insurance for children. More than 1.3 million children in the state were uninsured. And the number of children covered had declined from 1997 to 1999 in spite of the State Children's Health Insurance Program, or SCHIP, which had been created in 1997 for the specific purpose of providing federal money to the states to cover uninsured children of working families.

Jody Sakol had a particular knack for tracking down real people we could visit with at our policy events who could bring a human face to the issues we were tackling.

That visit to Houston was wrenching because we went to a community center in a low-income neighborhood and talked to people about the compromises they had been forced to make with their children's medical care. I remember Rosalinda Camarillo, who described powerfully why she had had to postpone surgery for her nine-year-old son. "We had to choose between paying for transportation to work and health insurance," she said.

I was sent to Texas four more times over the course of the 2000 campaign. We knew we'd never win the state, but it was the best place to contrast Bush's record and plans with ours. That's why I returned as part of the October offensive, this time standing in front of belching smokestacks at an oil refinery in West Texas, where the governor started his career. "Texas is our most air-toxic-polluted state," I told the assembled crowd. "Texas is number three in water pollution and, sadly, number one in air pollution."

Then I visited a small house in the shadow of another air-polluting refinery and spoke there with a group of women who were angry about the problems their children were having with asthma and frightened by the number of people in their neighborhood who had recently discovered they had cancer.

The next day we headed down to a dirt-poor town, one of the 1,400 *colonias* that mark the Texas-Mexico border. Most of the four hundred thousand residents of the *colonias* (roughly 85 percent are U.S. citizens) live without running water, sewer lines, dependable electricity, or paved roads. In nearly six years in office, Bush had never visited a single *colonia*. "You don't have to go to Alaska to know that it's cold," Bush's secretary of state, Elton Bomer, had protested in Bush's defense, "and I don't think you have to go to a *colonia* to know what it's like."

He was wrong. These visits to Texas left me with deep impressions, which I returned to in my speeches for the rest of the campaign, and in my work since.

No matter how critical I got, whenever I mentioned my opponents in a speech, I made certain to stress that I was talking about their records and proposals, not them. And from that rejected speech on, Paul took pains to insert what he came to describe as "classic Lieberman qualifiers"—"I'm troubled to say," "I'm really disappointed to tell you," and so on.

◈ *The New York Times* published an analysis of Joe's rhetoric that I thought was right on target. Richard Perez-Pena, a reporter who traveled on the *Spirit* throughout the campaign, wrote, "Mr. Lieberman has a rare talent for making attacks that do not come across as attacks," in a September 30 article chronicling Joe's "blistering assault" on the governor's Texas environmental record that Joe had made in a speech in Houston the day before. "His criticisms, often prefaced by phrases like 'I'm sorry to say,' or 'sadly,' and delivered with a litany of supporting detail, sound less like those of an aggressive politician than of a concerned neighbor leaning over a back fence, sharing a troubling bit of gossip."

Perez-Pena went on: "'He can deliver these pretty hard-hitting messages without any sense of rancor,' said Ross K. Baker, a professor of political science at Rutgers University, 'and have the listener walk away feeling like he was throwing garlands of flowers. It's a tremendous asset at a time when people are clearly tired of strident attacks.'"

Then he finished with another quote from Professor

Baker that really amused us—and our Catholic friends, too. "'[Lieberman] has almost a pastoral quality to him,' even when expressing an opinion strongly, Professor Baker said. 'If he were Roman Catholic, he'd be a great parish priest.'"

I'd lost only one election in my years in politics, and that was for the House in 1980. I was nineteen points ahead with a few weeks left in that race. A third of the voters were undecided. I'd been in the state senate for ten years, the last six as majority leader. My slogan was "Lieberman—a proven leader you can count on." The problem was that the more I campaigned, the more I realized that the last thing voters wanted in 1980 was a proven, or familiar, leader. They wanted a change. That's a big part of why they voted for Ronald Reagan that year.

I called my political consultant. "I think we're going at this all wrong. The voters want change."

Stay the course, he said. It's too late to change your message now. And besides, polling shows you way ahead.

I did what he said and I lost.

It was a painful experience, but it taught me some things. One is that the professional consultants are not always right. And others are that you've got to listen to the voters and follow your instincts. I applied those lessons again in the last month of the 2000 campaign.

When the debate with Dick Cheney was over, a new

chapter in the campaign was opening, and I stopped to reflect on how I wanted the final month to go. We were slipping in the polls. We were still doing well on health care, prescription drugs, and education, but we were merely holding our own on the economy, and we were getting *killed* on defense and values. I was a member of the Armed Services Committee, and I knew the Clinton administration had invested a lot to keep our defenses strong. As for values, they were my priority; it was a good part of why I was on the ticket.

Less than two weeks after my debate with Cheney, the second and third Gore-Bush debates came and went—October 11 at Wake Forest University in Winston-Salem, North Carolina, and a town hall–style debate October 17 in St. Louis, Missouri. Al later described himself as too hot in the first debate, too cold in the second, but *just right* in the third.

The election had become volatile. CNN had a daily tracking poll of public opinion that in one day could swing up or down fifteen points. This made no sense. Most of the steadier polls showed that for the first time since the convention, we'd lost the lead. At this critical point in the campaign, our message wasn't making it through to enough people. It was essential for us to figure out why it wasn't getting through and what we could do to clarify and sharpen it. In other words, how were we going to regain the lead?

Early in the campaign, in August, I'd said that I needed to understand where the campaign was and what its strategy would be. In response, a full-day meeting had been set up at a hotel in Washington with the whole campaign staff. Collectively, we'd taken a look at the big picture. It had been a terrific and productive session. It was also the last meeting of its kind that I attended. For the rest of the race, my staff just teleconferenced with Gore's staff in Nashville every day.

By October, it seemed to me we had to clarify and better communicate our policies in three critical areas: government, values, and the economy. First, it was clear from the polling data that the Republicans were making inroads by painting Gore as a big government liberal. An ad was running in seventeen decisive states that accused Al of "proposing three times the new spending President Clinton proposed, wiping out the entire surplus, and creating a deficit again." We needed to fight this accusation by stressing the Clinton-Gore record of fiscal responsibility, turning big federal deficits into big federal surpluses. We also needed to stress our more conservative handling of the large projected surplus than Bush's. We were going to spend one-third on middle-class tax cuts, one-third on investments in education and health care, and one-third to reduce our national debt or keep the budget balanced in case surplus projections didn't materialize. Bush and Cheney were going to spend more on tax cuts than we could be sure would be there in surplus to pay for it.

Second, the polls that Tom Nides showed me at the end of every week kept saying that voters believed our nation had "lost its moral bearings" and that they trusted the Republican ticket more than Gore and me to get us back on the right moral track. These survey results were maddening to me, because no matter what people might say about Al's campaign style or his position on a given issue, he was clearly a man of honor. As for me, well, connecting values to our politics was my priority and a good part of why I was put on the ticket.

I've been through enough campaigns to know that if you want to get an important message across to a lot of voters quickly, there's no substitute for putting that message into television commercials. So I told Nides, Eskew, and Greenberg, "This damn thing is so close, and we're so far behind on values, let's make some TV commercials that remind people that Al is a man of character and that stress the commitment to national and family values that he and I have."

Tom made the pitch, and Stan backed us. As lead pollster, he saw what happened each time we talked about religion and values. The numbers rose noticeably. "You can't talk enough about them," he had told me early on.

The campaign agreed to cut a commercial. With existing footage of Al and me together, a voice-over spoke of the way traditional American values were expressed in our lives and our policies. But the campaign strategists decided not to run the ad. When I asked why, I was told they focus-grouped it, and it got good reactions, but not as good as some other commercials on single issues. Their conclusion reminded me both of what I had learned from my defeat in 1980 and of something I said to Hadassah after my election to the Senate in 1988. "We couldn't have won if we didn't have the professional campaign consultants. But we wouldn't have won if we'd done everything they recommended." At some point you have to remember that politics is a profession where experience should have taught you some things about people, their needs, their frustrations, their hopes. My gut told me those values commercials would have helped. In retrospect, I wish I had gone to Al directly and insisted that they run.

Although Nashville decided not to do a commercial about Al's character and our shared commitment to values in public life, I stressed those themes in all my remaining campaigning. I also resolved that before the campaign ended I would give one more major speech on the importance of faith in American life.

The third policy challenge of the fall of 2000—what to say about the economy—should have been the easiest, because the economy had boomed so beautifully during the Clinton-Gore years. But it wasn't. I blame that on the closeness of the race and Ralph Nader's candidacy. The most logical formulation on the economy would have been: Do the American people want to keep moving forward, building on the progress and prosperity of the Clinton-Gore administration with Gore and Lieberman, or do they want to slide backward with Bush and Cheney to the days of overspending our budget, causing ballooning debt, higher interest rates, and higher unemployment?

The closeness of the race must have convinced our consultants that we needed to make sharper, more confrontational economic distinctions. So did the Nader candidacy, which was buoyed, also by the closeness of the race, into hoping Ralph might take enough votes from us to throw some pivotal states like Oregon to Bush. Nader's message was very anti-business and very unfair: "When it comes to corporate power," he told a New York audience, "the only difference between Gore and Bush is the velocity with which their knees hit the floor when corporations bang on the door."

That rhetoric was outrageous, but I'm afraid it pressured our campaign to meet the challenge in words that sometimes sounded stridently anti-business. That might have helped to bring back some votes from Nader, but I fear it pushed away many more middle-class voters and investors whom we needed to win.

I often find myself quoting my law school classmate and friend, the late senator Paul Tsongas, who once said, "You can't be pro-jobs and anti-business, because it's business that creates most of the jobs." That's why I'm comfortable calling myself a pro-business Democrat. By 2000, I could add that business created not only jobs, but wealth for tens of millions of middle-class Americans who own stock directly or in mutual funds, 401(k)s, or other retirement plans.

Needless to say, being pro-business doesn't mean you believe individual businesses or business people can do no wrong, as I found when I was attorney general of Connecticut and regularly sued businesses that cheated consumers or polluted the environment. We've all seen that again more recently in the Enron and other corporate accounting scandals.

It's just as unfair to suggest that businesses are all wrong as it is to suggest that they're never wrong. That's the misunderstanding that was encouraged, I thought, by the phrase "the people vs. the powerful" that was heard in our campaign. That's why I didn't use it. I thought it suggested an economic class conflict for pieces of a limited pie that is not what the American economy is about. We have always sought to expand our national pie to employ and feed more people. That certainly was the reality during the Clinton–Gore administration.

It was also not the balanced view of the relationship between business and government that, I am convinced, is shared by a majority of the American people. They understand that it is unfair to be reflexively against business because business creates jobs and wealth for them and their families, but they also want government to be ready and willing to fight on their behalf when individual businesses, including big businesses, treat them unfairly.

So in the campaign, when I talked of the priority a Gore-Lieberman administration would give to environmental protection, I spoke about the importance of tough law enforcement against polluters but also about big and small businesses that had embraced the environmental ethic and voluntarily spent billions of dollars cleaning up their operations.

When I talked about the help seniors needed in paying for prescription drugs, I always said I was not against the pharmaceutical industry. After all, they were producing drugs that were keeping us all alive and well for a lot longer. That didn't mean we had to accept drug-pricing policies that were unfair.

My audiences, including the big Democratic rally crowds, responded positively to this approach. Incidentally, Al Gore's record as a senator and vice president shows it had also been his approach.

Most Americans don't dislike the rich and powerful. They just want to be treated fairly by them, and one day they want to be rich and powerful themselves.

◈ Joe needed a trusted adviser. Every candidate needs one, someone you go back with a long way, a battle-tested friend. Someone who will let you be you but will also be straight with you when you need to face hard truths—and that's even more rare. Al Gore's brother-in-law, Frank Hunger, played that role for Al, but for the first half of the campaign, Joe didn't have anyone like that around. And then we invited Al From to join us on the road.

⧈ Al From has been my sounding board and valued source of ideas since I met him in 1987, when I was deciding whether to run for the Senate and when the organization he had founded, the Democratic Leadership Council, was only two years old. He had started it as an idea center, a group that could serve as a catalyst to move the Democratic Party beyond the old left-right debate. He wanted to galvanize support for a more centrist public philosophy of new ideas—one that stressed three essential values: opportunity for all, responsibility from all, and a community of all Americans.

Bill Clinton was a former DLC chairman, and his embrace of the New Democratic philosophy helped make him the only Democrat to be elected president since the 1960s, with the exception of Jimmy Carter (who was to a great degree elected because he wasn't tainted by Watergate). When Al Gore picked me to be his running mate, I was serving as DLC chairman.

◈ We were on our way to Detroit. After takeoff, I got up from my seat next to Joe, walked back to Al From, and said, "Why don't you go sit with him? Maybe the two of you can figure out a few things he ought to be saying." Together, they started rethinking everything—what points needed to be stressed, what Joe needed to do for the ticket to win.

When we asked Al to join us on the plane, we didn't realize he would wind up pretty much sticking around

until Election Day—but that's what he did, and thank God for it. His role, he told me, was to make sure that Joe could be Joe.

With Paul Orzulak, Al and I revised my standard speech, line by line, issue by issue. Tina Flournoy had told me, "When you accept the role of vice president, you necessarily give up a lot of your ability to navigate independently," and I certainly understood that. But I also felt there was a way to follow my heart and head while still fulfilling the needs and desires of the Gore campaign.

We brought values back as a primary theme—and linked it to a message of economic growth. I visited high-tech businesses and spoke about the new economy, and I arranged to speak out again soon on the important and constructive role religion has played and can play in American life. True to the tripartite DLC mantra of opportunity, responsibility, community, we decided my standard stump speech should open with the theme of "opportunity." I'd begin by discussing my grandparents and why they came to this country. The great promise of America is that if you work hard and play by the rules, if you're "responsible," you ought to be able to go as far as your God-given ability will take you. Then I'd contrast the great record of the Clinton-Gore administration with Bush's record in Texas. I'd offer a line I'd heard from my Senate colleague and friend Tom Harkin: "About all you need to know about this election," I'd tell crowds, "is what you learned when you learned to drive a car. You know: If you want to go backward, put it in *R.* And if you want to go forward, put it in *D.*"

By this point in the campaign, I'd delivered so many speeches that except for formal occasions, I no longer needed a text. A list of talking points that I could pick and choose from served just as well. To provide a glimpse of the shape of my new stump speech, here are some of those talking points:

- We are blessed to live in the first nation in the history of the world that was founded not just on a set of borders, but a set of ideals—that here in America, if you work hard, play by the rules, and try to teach your kids right from wrong, you should be able to rise as high as your God-given talents will take you.
- Eight years ago, even though people were working hard, they were having a hard time getting by. Bill Clinton and Al Gore ran for the White House in 1992 because they believed they could get America moving. Their mission was to fight for people and to expand opportunity, not to expand government.
- Eight years later, instead of losing jobs, we have 22 million new jobs.
- Instead of failing businesses, we have four million new businesses.
- Instead of the largest deficit in history, we have the largest surplus in history.

- Instead of the biggest government ever, we have the smallest government in 40 years.
- Instead of exploding welfare rolls, we have cut the welfare rolls in half.
- Instead of rising crime, we have the lowest crime rate in 25 years.
- Instead of a triple-dip recession, we have the strongest economy in the 224-year history of the United States of America.
- The question in this election is simple: Do we want to go back to the failed ideas of the past? Or do we want to build on our progress with new ideas for the future? I don't know about you: I don't want to go back to the days of deficit and debt. I don't want to go back to the days of crime and unemployment. I don't want to go back to the days of high interest rates with George Bush. I want to go forward with Al Gore.
- Our opponent has been governor of Texas for six years. Today, he says he wants to do for America what he has done in Texas.
- But Texas today has some of the dirtiest air in America. It has 1.4 million children who don't have health insurance. It's government spending has grown at twice the rate of the federal government. And according to the nonpartisan Rand Institute: The gap in scores between white and black students isn't improving, it's growing. Yet, last year, Governor Bush declared the need for a tax cut for big oil companies an emergency.

- I don't know about you: I don't want Governor Bush to do to America what he has done to Texas.
- On November 7th, people need to understand: There are real differences between us.
- Governor Bush wants to give a $1.6 trillion tax cut, 43 percent of which goes to the top 1 percent. He's also promising $1.1 trillion to seniors. He's promising the same $1.1 trillion to younger workers to privatize Social Security. He's also promising to invest in education, prescription drugs, and defense.
- The problem is, his numbers don't add up. To do it all, we're going to have to put more than $1 trillion back on America's credit card.
- Don't take my word for it. The respected, nonpartisan American Academy of Actuaries said last week that the Bush plan will bring a return to federal budget deficits and "make it all but impossible to pay off the national debt."
- In his speeches, Governor Bush says that we spend more than he does. It's not true. The academy spokesman said point-blank: "Bush is very much overspending Gore."
- In this election, I am proud that the Democratic Party can now say what we couldn't have said 15 years ago: We are the party of fiscal discipline and economic growth.
- Al Gore and I know that government didn't create this prosperity, the American people did. Government shouldn't get in the way of what the private sector does

best. But there are things we can do to create the conditions to expand opportunity, not government.

- We want to help make college more affordable by making the first $10,000 of college tuition tax deductible.
- We want to do right by our parents and grandparents by expanding Medicare to cover the high cost of prescription drugs.
- We want to cut taxes for middle-class families, not just the wealthiest 1 percent.
- We want to finish the job of cutting crime by putting another 50,000 community police officers on the streets.
- We want to go to the next stage of welfare reform by making fathers take responsibility for the kids they bring into this world.
- We want to do all we can to make our public schools the best in the world.
- We are going to do something else George Bush and Dick Cheney won't do: we are going to protect and defend a woman's right to choose.
- We are going to do all we can to stand with parents as they stand against the violence and vulgarity in our culture.
- In the end, this isn't just about priorities, it's about values. The values of faith, family, opportunity, responsibility, and community should inspire and inform the choices we make as a nation. We are lucky to have a candidate whose faith and whose values guide not just his life, but his priorities. The closer people look at this elec-

tion, the more they will conclude: Al Gore is the best man for the job.

- For 224 years, America has dreamed bigger dreams and tried bolder solutions than any other nation. Now is not the time to settle for anything less than the best that we can be. Give us your hands, your hearts, your voices, and your votes. Together, we will make the future of this good and great country even brighter.

I felt that I was closing strong, wrapping the campaign's major themes in my own package of priorities and principles. I was delighted; Al From, my senate staff, and my campaign staff were delighted; and so were the crowds. Even Nashville seemed happy. When I'd come on board, I had promised to do the best I could to get Al Gore elected president. In October, I felt I was fulfilling that promise, my way.

CHAPTER ELEVEN

◈ It's Saturday morning and Tom McCarthy is waiting outside our house. He's serious in the way Secret Service agents tend to be. He's wearing that earpiece radio, polarized sunglasses, and shiny black tie-up shoes. And he says, "Okay, Senator, Mrs. Lieberman. I've got my *kippah* in my pocket, I'm ready to walk to shul."

◘ By October, I suspect, looking for the Lieberman parade was becoming a regular Saturday morning activity in Georgetown. Our synagogue is a mile-and-a-half walk from home, and you become fairly conspicuous when your small family is accompanied by a dozen agents as well as three or four state-of-the-art black SUVs. Every Saturday that we were in Washington, the agents charted a new route for us. Often neighbors and fellow congregants found us. They'd ask, "Can we join you?" Of course, we'd say, and our caravan to Kesher Israel, the Georgetown synagogue, would grow even longer.

At first our agents stood out in the synagogue in their "white silk, bar mitzvah–special *kippahs* [skullcaps]," as a friend described them. They aren't the kind worn by the regulars, but in time the Kesher Israel congregants offered them knit skullcaps with attached hair clips so the agents could blend in more easily. In fact, after a while the Secret Service became "virtually" indistinguishable, our friend said—quite an accomplishment for our very diverse group of agents.

One of the greatest gifts my parents gave me is Sabbath observance. I grew up with it, left it behind during my college and law school years, and then returned enthusiastically to it after my children were born. To paraphrase an old Jewish maxim, it is not so much that I keep the Sabbath as the Sabbath keeps me. It sustains me. The fourth of the Ten Commandments ("Remember the Sabbath day to sanctify it—for in six days God made the heavens and the earth . . . and all that is in them, and God rested on the seventh day.") is the reason the Sabbath is observed. And when we observe it, we are declaring that the earth and our lives are no accident, but the result of God's willful creation. It is a day for gratitude and regeneration through prayer and rest. It is a day set apart from the week for family and friends.

I once saw a bumper sticker that said, "Relax, the Sabbath is coming!" That sums up a lot of what I feel about God's day. The busier I have become, the more critical Sabbath observance has become to me for reasons that are not only spiritual but physical and, as the bumper sticker suggests, psychological. It helps me work harder and with more focus during the week knowing that the Sabbath is coming. And the Sabbath also reminds me what I should be working for on the other six days of the week.

On the campaign trail, adrenaline keeps you going; catnaps on the plane or in a car help, too. But sometimes the fatigue would go deep inside me. Then Shabbat comes and I am renewed and ready to go again.

During one private moment in the 2000 campaign, Al Gore, who takes his religion seriously, told me that earlier in his career he had thought about not doing any political events on Sunday. Now, watching my Sabbath observance, Al said, made him wish he had done it. He knew he couldn't suddenly stop working on Sundays in the middle of the campaign. But he said, "You know, if we get elected, I'm going to really think about it."

"That would be great, Al," I joked. "You watch the store on Saturday and I'll watch it on Sunday."

Hadassah, Hani, and I came together for most of the Sabbaths during the campaign. And we would try to link up with the rest of our family, too. I remember vividly our first Sabbath on the campaign trail. It was just after the Democratic National Convention, when we were on the Mississippi riverboat trip with the Gores. As Al danced up a storm at a party for Tipper's fifty-second birthday (campaign reporters were their special guests), Hadassah, Matt, Becca, Hani, and I were having the sweet experience of spending the Sabbath in La Crosse, Wisconsin.

A Lubavitch rabbi from Minnesota had brought kosher food to our hotel. (Throughout the campaign and across the country, Lubavitch rabbis kindly, generously, left kosher food for us at our hotels. We were very grateful. But our whereabouts were supposed to be classified and confidential. We and our Secret Service agents wondered: How did they find us?) On Saturday morning, as we walked to the local synagogue, La Crosse residents emerged from their homes to greet us. This was small-town America, and though we were far from home, we felt we *were* home. When we left services at the synagogue, a combination of the local Conservative and Reform Jewish communities, the rabbi walked us to the door and said he hoped we'd come again—because he'd had a larger attendance that morning than on Yom Kippur.

When Shabbat comes, you walk. You're just another person, observing your faith, doing what it is you do on Friday nights and Saturdays. So wherever you are, you become more accessible to people.

This means you get to have conversations you might not otherwise have. In Portland, Oregon, I attended services at a lovely temple and afterward dropped in on the social hour for a quick visit. As I was walking out, a woman close to my age stopped me.

"I've got to talk to you about something," she said conspiratorially.

I let her take me aside.

"I've seen your mother on TV," she said. "She's *adorable.*"

I said, Well, thank you, I think so, too.

She leaned in closer. "I want to introduce her to my father. He's a *great* dancer."

My then eighty-five-year-old mother loved that story, although the match has not yet been made.

My campaign staff came to appreciate Shabbat; they needed down time, too. But I wondered how they felt about the Jewish Holidays that all fell in the weeks before the election. There was Rosh Hashanah (September 30–October 1), Yom Kippur (October 9), Sukkot (October 14–15), Shemini Atseret (October 21), and Simchat Torah (October 22).

"The Jewish High Holidays haven't attracted this much attention in America since Sandy Koufax decided not to pitch on Yom Kippur," Jeffrey Weiss wrote in the *Dallas Morning News.* The comparison to the great Koufax was right up there with Tony Bennett complimenting my singing among the greater (self-delusional) personal moments of the campaign.

The week following Rosh Hashanah, the Jewish New Year, is spent in soul-searching and repentance, and it culminates in the most holy of days, Yom Kippur, the Day of Atonement. This marks the end of the penitent period, from which we hope to emerge with a feeling of confidence and faith. This can be very powerful fuel for a candidate embroiled in a tough race. Nevertheless, if there had been a few religiously observant Jewish American Founding Fathers, presidential elections would have been scheduled some other time of the year.

◈ **Sukkot was coming, and I just said, "Joe, Joe, this is too much." We were supposed to be on the campaign trail the first two days and last two days of the holiday—and those are the days when you're not supposed to work—so we would start campaigning right after sundown in these two major battleground states, but we were also supposed to put up the sukkah at home, and I said, "This is ridiculous, we can't do it all."**

And Joe said, "All right, we'll skip it this year. We'll use our neighbor's sukkah instead."

A sukkah is a hut, or a booth, you put up next to your house, and you "dwell" in it—which is to say, you eat your meals in it, although some people even sleep in it. The significance of the holiday goes back to the Bible, to Leviticus 23: 42–43: " . . . in huts you are to stay for seven days . . . in order that your generations may know that in huts I had the Children of Israel stay when I brought them out of the land of Egypt, I am the Lord your God!" In other words, the sukkot that we build remind us of the forty years spent wandering in the desert. They're intentionally temporary: when you sit in them you should be able to look up and see the stars, and if it rains, you should feel it come down.

◘ We "dwell" in the sukkah to remind ourselves of the fragility of life, of the uncertainties we face, of how much we depend on God's grace, and we remind ourselves as well of our modest place in the Universe. Always a valuable reminder for a politician.

◈ Ethan and Ariela had worked on a Habitat for Humanity project when we were all in Kentucky for the vice presidential debate. When they heard that we might not put up our sukkah, they e-mailed us. "Building a house in Kentucky . . . ," Ariela wrote, "I thought about the importance of owning a home as part of the American dream. The holiday reminds us how important housing and shelter are, and how lucky most of us are to have solid homes."

"You have no choice," Ethan argued. "You have to put it up." Besides, he added as a clincher, Sukkot is the time when our ancestors brought their last harvest to the temple as an expression of gratitude. As a family, we had so much to be grateful for.

So we stayed in D.C. for Sukkot, and up went the

sukkah, the temporary booth, right next to another temporary booth—the one that the Secret Service had built behind our house for its agents. The agents never said anything about it, but God only knows what they were thinking: These Liebermans, they're finally home for a few days, and look at them—they're sitting outside, eating their meals in some leaky hut!

A few days later, we introduced them to Simchat Torah, the joyous day when we celebrate the completion of the annual cycle of weekly Torah readings. We get to the end, to Moses' farewell speech and death, and then we immediately scroll back to the beginning to be read all over again—starting, of course, with Genesis. But before we do, the Torah is carried around the synagogue seven times, with everybody singing and dancing, and then it's placed back in the ark.

A congregant observed our Secret Service agents trying to balance ancient ritual with contemporary security practices. "Because of space constraints," he wrote, "Kesher always arranges to have the block of N Street in front of the *shul* cordoned off to permit room for dancing with the Torahs. The agents had to run dogs up and down the streets, searching every parked car. Meanwhile all the Liebermans danced. The agents, some anxious but amused, positioned themselves around the circles [of dancers] so they were never more than six or seven feet away from them."

If there was one misunderstanding of my personal philosophy that really bothered me in the course of the campaign, it was this: I don't feel you have to be a religious person to be a moral person. Certainly there are many nonreligious people I know who are good people and many religious ones who are not.

But I do believe that accountability to a "higher authority" helps people develop a sense of right and wrong, and an appreciation for justice and mercy. The Ten Commandments and the other lessons from the Bible that tell us God cares about how we behave help us answer the questions that test us every day: Why is it wrong to lie or cheat or steal? Why is it wrong to use violence to settle conflicts? Why is it wrong to be unfaithful to one's spouse or to exploit children? To defraud a customer? To despoil the environment?

When you think about it, strengthening Medicare and Social Security follows the commandment to honor our fathers and mothers. Improving our schools and expanding access to health care fulfills our obligations to our children, the most precious of God's creations. And protecting the environment is a way to protect and guard God's natural creation.

This is something I feel very strongly: God has entrusted us with this world, and it is our sacred obligation to take care of it, to improve it, even to try to perfect it.

If anyone knew about my long-term commitment to the environment, it was Ralph Nader. I've known Ralph a long time. He's from Winsted, Connecticut, and we've known each other since the early days. There was a time when Ralph was a hero to me; I admired this gutsy crusader for consumers and the environment. So it was ironic, to say the least, when Nader, running for president on the Green Party ticket, began turning up in environmentally conscious states declaring there was no significant difference between the Gore-Lieberman and Bush-Cheney tickets.

No difference when it came to oil drilling in the Arctic National Wildlife Refuge? No difference regarding global warming or clean air or clean water regulations? Mining in our national forests? Arsenic in our drinking water? Protection of our great natural spaces?

"For twenty-four years, I have never backed down or given up on the environment, and I never will in my whole life! I guaran-damn-tee-it," Al declared to a crowd of more than thirty thousand in Madison, Wisconsin, in late October.

Wisconsin had become one of those states where Nader posed a real threat to us. It wasn't, of course, that he could win it, but the danger in some traditionally Democratic states was that he would lure enough voters from us to tip those states to Bush. In Oregon, for example, Nader was polling over 10 percent of the voters—most of whom had not, I would guess, thought of voting for George W. Bush. And it wasn't just in Oregon and Wisconsin that "the Nader factor" was creating problems. Washington State, Minnesota, Maine, New Hampshire, New Mexico—those electoral votes were all at stake. Meanwhile, we were neck and neck in Pennsylvania, Ohio, Michigan, and Missouri. We could not afford to give up a single vote, and Nader knew it.

So did the Republicans. In the Pacific Northwest, they put their money behind ads that showed Nader lambasting Gore. Nader, Bush, and Cheney—the ultimate strange bedfellows! For his part, Ralph tried out the argument that the election of Bush-Cheney might actually serve as a catalyst for good. "A bumbling Texas governor would galvanize the environmental community as never before," he told Melinda Henneberger of *The New York Times.* "The Sierra Club doubled its membership under James Watt." As my mom would say, "Don't do me any favors."

The Sierra Club didn't see it the way Nader did. Neither did the League of Conservation Voters. Both began ad campaigns directed at the Nader voter, warning of the environmental consequences if Bush was elected. Similarly, the Human Rights Campaign and People for the American Way began campaigns warning that a Bush win could swing the Supreme Court drastically to the right, and the National Abortion and Reproductive Rights Action League (NARAL) spent $1.5 million in TV ads in the Pacific North-

Joe and Hadassah at the rainy rally in Minneapolis. To the left is one of our favorite campaign signs: "Batman, Superman, Lieberman."

west and five other states, sounding the alarm about what would happen to a woman's right to choose if Bush and Cheney were elected. (In the end, twice as many men as women supported Nader.)

Ralph's presence in the race meant that we were forced to redirect our energies and resources (money!) in the final month of the campaign. Nader had put different states into play, and he forced us to fight different battles.

In the final few weeks of the campaign, I was sent to every state where Nader was doing well. In direct appeals to people thinking of voting for Ralph, I stressed the Gore-Lieberman commitment to protect the environment and a woman's right to choose—both of which would be endangered if Bush and Cheney were elected and both of which, I thought, mattered a lot to voters leaning to Nader.

It wasn't simply that a vote for Nader was a vote for Bush, I told voters. It was more than that. Thinking voters would be untrue to their personal principles and priorities if they voted for Nader because their vote would be going to elect men who didn't share their values and beliefs on environmental protection and a woman's right to choose, and in fact would undermine them. (Looking back, I wasn't wrong, was I?)

I have always believed that politics is ultimately about ideas and that you win elections by convincing a majority of the voters that your ideas—your vision of the future—is better for them than your opponent's. That's what I was trying to convince the potential Nader voters. In the final two weeks of the campaign, I had two other parts of our vision of the future that I wanted to speak to voters about in a serious way: national security and shared values and faith.

National security. At the University of Pittsburgh branch at Greensburg, I spoke about the imperative of American leadership in the world, about the importance of sustaining a muscular, values-based foreign policy, about the impressive record of the Clinton-Gore administration in spreading freedom's range and mediating regional conflicts, and about how well prepared Al Gore was to continue to protect our national security and advance our values.

When I finished my speech in Greensburg that day and the applause began, my granddaughter Tennessee bolted from her mother April's arms and ran up on the stage, shouting, "Poppy!" I swept her up in a big hug and felt an internal explosion of grandfatherly love that surprised me. I had missed the kids a lot. And maybe Tennessee's surprise appearance personalized for me what I had just said about how important it is to protect the future security of the American people, including, most particularly, America's children.

Shared values and faith. I wanted to go back to that one more time.

In the two months since I had preached at Reverend Wendell Anthony's Fellowship Chapel in Detroit, attitudes had softened toward my public statements of faith. My staff had gotten used to them; the Anti-Defamation League had been reprimanded for overreacting to them;

the media was bored with them; and our pollsters agreed it had potential to attract undecided voters in this very close election. So even though Nashville had chosen not to focus on values in paid television commercials, they supported my plan to make one last serious speech about the importance of faith in American society today. The last time I had tried to tackle this issue, my message had been obscured by controversy. But I truly felt I had an important point to make—one that needed to be said to as broad an audience as possible.

I turned to my scheduler, Ryan Montoya. What an enormous job that is, national campaign scheduler—and Ryan did it superbly. I told Ryan I wanted to make a significant speech about faith and values in a significant location. Ryan was a young man, just twenty-five years old, whose unusual name is explained by the fact that his mother is Irish American and his father is Mexican American. I know exactly where you ought to give your speech, he said.

And so, on October 24, I spoke before almost six hundred students and faculty members at Ryan Montoya's alma mater—one of the leading Roman Catholic educational institutions in the United States, the University of Notre Dame in South Bend, Indiana.

The speech I gave that day was a personal manifesto. Drawing from the Torah, the New Testament, and the Qur'an, I called for a renewal of the moral and cultural life of America.

I told the assembly in Washington Hall that despite "our material abundance, there is a persistent sense, which I share, of unease about our moral future. As people peer into the national looking glass, they don't like the reflection of our values they see: the continued breakdown of our families, the coarsening of our public life, the pollution of our culture, the erosion of classroom discipline, and the explosion of gunfire in our schoolyards."

What we desperately need now, I said, is to "rebuild our moral consensus," and the way to do that is to "take our religious beliefs and values, our sense of justice, our sense of right and wrong, into America's cultural and communal life." I repeated what I said back in Detroit at Reverend Anthony's church: that the Founding Fathers were men of profound faith, but that in recent years our society had become so intent on separating church from state, "we practically banish religious values and religious institutions from our public life."

Prohibiting the "establishment" of any one religion and protecting the free exercise of all religions is a precious central tenet of American life, but that does not mean that we must exclude faith from the public square. I wondered whether that exclusion was part of the reason too many Americans seem incapable today of "making moral judgments which are critical to the functioning of a free society."

"We Americans have got to have faith," I declared. "Faith and the values that flow from it were central to the founding of this country. They have always shaped and stirred our national conscience. . . . [Our] best hope for rekindling the American spirit and renewing our common values is to have faith again. Not just in our hearts, but in our communities; not just in our private places of worship, but in our public spaces of conversation; and not just in our separate beliefs, but in our common commitment to our common purpose."

I made it clear that these values are not "exclusive to any one faith or any one denomination." In fact, we have become a country in which some of the larger differences of opinion are no longer between different religions, but between believers and nonbelievers.

So what role should the government play? I made clear that the government couldn't and shouldn't try to solve our moral problems itself. "And that's because in our democracy, where our first principle is freedom, government cannot and must not try to control all of our behavior. It cannot force us to love and honor parents. It cannot force us to treat our neighbors with respect, to care for those in need. Nor can it nourish our souls or do the rudimentary work of teaching us right from wrong. Those responsibilities have been and always will be entrusted to our traditional transmitters of values: religion, the family, and that broad range of civic organizations that collectively form the sinews of what we call civil society."

But the leaders of government can set an example by their behavior and establish a tone with their words. "Vice President Gore and I share this commitment to a higher purpose," I declared. "We share this vision of a more just, more moral, more inclusive America. And we share a dedication to using our offices and our influence to support and encourage this new burst of moral and cultural renewal. We want to continue to build partnerships with faith-based organizations and other community groups around America that are succeeding in repairing our frayed social and human fabric. We want to continue standing by parents who are trying to protect their children from the moral toxins that are polluting our culture. . . .

"Vice President Gore and I want to bring truth to power. The truth of faith and the power of values that flow from it. We cannot cure our moral ailments from Washington, this we know. But we can exert leadership from our public pulpits and exhort the American people to realize their best ideals in their lives and in the life of the American community."

I had learned my lesson earlier in the campaign. Before I delivered this speech at Notre Dame, it had been sent to Nashville. No objections were heard. And while it was nationally televised and fairly widely covered, there was no controversy this time.

I had spoken from my heart, and with just two weeks to go before Election Day, I hoped that my words would provide a bridge for our ticket to some of the remaining undecided voters in this increasingly close campaign. But most of all, I was proud of what I had said because I believed it so deeply.

I vividly remembered how shaken Tom Nides had been

after the speech in Detroit, how worried he'd been that I'd alienated voters. This time, he watched the speech on television, from a distant state, but he called a few minutes after it was over. I could hear the excitement in his voice. "Beautiful job, Senator," he said. Two months in a presidential campaign is a very long time.

CHAPTER TWELVE

"If we win it here, we'll win it *everywhere*! It's up to you, Florida, Florida!" That's what I sang to the enthusiastic Floridians in my best takeoff on Sinatra at the sunset rally at Miami-Dade Community College. It was Monday, October 23. The election was two weeks from tomorrow. I'd started the day breakfasting and praying with ministers in a restaurant in the heavily African American Liberty City section of Miami. Then I'd moved on to a wonderfully welcoming rally of Haitian Americans, which was followed by another rousing rally with a thousand people at the Aventura Turnberry Jewish Center; a visit to the grave of Jorge Mas Canosa, the late leader of anti-Castro Cuban Americans, who had become a valued friend and steadfast supporter of mine; and then to a meeting with Cuban American leaders at the Freedom Tower, the old building where Cuban immigrants had been processed when they arrived in America, now being rebuilt in gratitude by the community. As I spoke, I stood in front of a grand mural that had been painted during the 1930s and included a nude woman over whom my alert advance team had temporarily painted a bathing suit.

That was Florida in all its diversity. And that was one reason I so enjoyed campaigning in the Sunshine State—which was fortunate, because I was spending an awful lot of time there. "Six months ago, nobody thought we'd be close in Florida," I declared at a rally when I returned a week later, but "it is a dead heat here in Florida, and the momentum is in our direction!"

It was true: Democrats had originally written off Florida and its twenty-five electoral votes. Governor Jeb Bush was clearly going to do what he could to deliver the state to his brother. In addition, the Cuban American community was furious with Clinton over Elian Gonzalez, and its anger was spilling over to hurt Gore. But now, in spite of those factors, and in spite of the fact that the Republicans had far outspent the Democrats in the state, Florida was looking as though it might be ours.

I had told Al we could do it.

When he interviewed me over breakfast at the Naval Observatory in June, and asked me why he should choose me, I talked about my experience, our similar records, our friendship—and then added that I thought I could help attract moderate independent voters concerned about values throughout America, as well as voters in states with large ethnic populations such as New York, New Jersey, Pennsylvania, Illinois, Michigan, and California. I particularly remember saying, "I am confident I can help you win Florida."

I was hopeful about Florida not just because it had a large Jewish population. A booming high-tech corridor had grown up between Orlando and Tampa, and as a pro-business, pro-growth Democrat, I had built a good relationship with that community. And then there were the Cuban Americans.

It was a strange twist of fate that brought me close to the Florida Cuban community. It happened when I ran for the Senate in 1988. Lowell Weicker liked to vacation in Cuba. In fact, he liked to scuba dive there with Fidel Castro. The relationship between Castro and Weicker drove the Cubans in Miami crazy, and so did Weicker's voting record on Cuba. When I chose to run against the senator, the Cubans adopted me.

They're a great community. I feel close to them. They've worked hard and have done well, and they really are "patriotic Americans." That's why, throughout the campaign, I kept pressing to campaign in the Cuban communities in Florida. I particularly wanted to go to Little Havana in Miami. I'd seen polls that showed we were getting only about 10 percent of the Cuban vote, and I'd say, What's going on? Send me in there. It can't get any worse, and the ticket deserves better.

The Cuban community is not a traditional Democratic base, and I'm afraid some in Nashville saw them as right-wing extremists to be avoided. The campaign was also reluctant to reopen the Elian Gonzalez affair. But, given that a large voting bloc was at stake in a critically important state, Nashville's resistance seemed bizarre to me. Tom

Nides saw my relationship with the Cubans as a political headache. We'd schedule something with the Cubans, he'd change the plan. It took me until the last Saturday of the campaign to make it to Little Havana. Meanwhile, as I was trying to push through the Nashville wall to get to the Cubans, some of the leaders of the community were getting enormous pressure to keep me out. That led to the carefully orchestrated visits to Jorge Mas Canosa's grave with his family and to the Freedom Tower with a larger group from the community. I will never forget the loyal friendship they showed me, even though they were under pressure from Jeb Bush to stay away from me. That's why someone suggested the graveside visit; it gave Mas Canosa's family and friends a nonpolitical place to be with me.

At least a dozen states were still too close to call, but few were as tight—or as critical—as Florida. Bush was all over the state, and so were we. By the end of the campaign, we were spending about $1 million a week on advertising in Florida, and the Bush campaign was still spending at least 50 percent more than we were. *Washington Post* correspondent David Von Drehle reported a week before the election that there was "an unprecedented absentee ballot campaign" going on in the state. Little did I know at the time how important it would be.

"Election supervisors in counties across the state say

they are drowning in record numbers of requests," he wrote. "The Republicans struck first: Their Florida voters received letters from Gov. Jeb Bush with an easy-to-use perforated postcard attached. Just sign it and drop it in the mail to receive an absentee ballot.

"Democrats answered with their own simple postcard for their faithful voters. They no doubt recalled the 1988 Senate race here, when Democrat Buddy McKay went to bed on election night certain of victory, only to find the next morning that absentees had put Republican Connie Mack over the top."

We knew it was coming down to individual votes. Wherever he went, Al reminded voters that JFK won the White House by an average of *one vote* per precinct. Just "get me one more vote in each of your precincts," he exhorted in the final days of his campaign. "Your one vote is more powerful . . . than the voice of any powerful interest."

The list of battleground states was long. In the final two weeks, Al went to fifteen states. I visited sixteen, but believe me, I wasn't the only Lieberman out there.

◈ Anyone with any strain of Lieberman blood went to work. Matt was busy campaigning; Ethan was out there. So were Joe's ladies—Becca, April, Ariela, Baba (that's Joe's mother), sisters Rietta and Ellen, sister-in-law Judy and niece Elizabeth—and even the grandkids. We had a passionate commitment to one another, to the issues,

and most of all, to campaigning for Joe. So we put together the Lieberman Ladies' Tour. We got entertainment stars to join us—the wonderful Susan Dey from *L.A. Law,* the great actress Cicely Tyson. Melissa Etheridge kicked it off at a rally at Oakland University in Detroit at the end of October. I'll never forget the image of Becca dancing with our granddaughter Tennessee to Melissa's rock and roll.

It may all sound star-studded and luxurious, and part of it was, but part of it wasn't. I remember rushing to a beauty parlor in Columbia, Missouri, before going onstage at the Déjà Vu Club with Bob Weir of the Grateful Dead. Or stuck in a dark and narrow hallway, trying to juggle all the demands of the campaign, being interviewed about all the juggling that women do in their lives. . . .

The tour became a logistical challenge for our advance teams, because we all split up and fanned out across the country. April and the kids climbed on Joe's plane, then spun off with Baba, Ellen, and Rietta. Judy and Elizabeth joined me on my plane, and Becca and Ariela put together their own Lieberman show. The schedulers had us all going from 7:00 A.M. until 1:00 A.M. At one point, I was sitting in a slip in my hotel room, my hair up in curlers, doing early morning drive-time radio. Later that morning, MSNBC reporter Ann Thompson came by to film me. "How are you feeling?" she asked.

"Oh God," I groaned, "all I really want to do is to stay in my nightgown, and get into bed with my remote and

watch TV!" (A lot of people came up to me after this aired to encourage me to hang in there and keep going.)

There comes a point in every political race when the campaign starts being mostly about voter turnout. You still hope to reach the undecided voters with your message, but your organization must concentrate on those voters you know you've got and those leaning in your direction. You need to reach out to the people whose help you're going to need to bring them out on Election Day: the state and the city Democratic campaign organizations, the labor movement, the vast network of African American political leaders and churches across the country, Hispanic political and community leaders, and, recently, the gay and lesbian communities. Tina Flournoy once told me, "You think Bill Clinton won only because of his ideas. Well, his ideas did drive people to this obscure governor out of Arkansas. But he got the votes because he got the turnout, and he got the turnout because he had people like Harold Ickes on his team, people who had a lifelong connection to labor and a strong level of comfort with minority groups."

I agreed with what Tina was saying. But I also know—and Clinton does, too—that the right idea can ignite a campaign. And the wrong idea can hijack it—right up until the end.

I saw a hijacking forming at a critical event in Saginaw, Michigan. It was a town hall meeting later in October.

We'd already been to events that day in Detroit, Pontiac, and Flint and had met with representatives of the important labor unions in Michigan, particularly, of course, the United Automobile Workers (UAW). Here, a guy stood up and said, "I'm the leader of a union. I'm working really hard for you guys. But I can't tell you how often my members say to me, I'm not voting for Gore, because if Gore gets to be president he's going to take my guns away."

Now, I had been through this before in Connecticut, and Al had been through it in Tennessee. But this fellow was making a powerful point: The Republicans, with the help of the National Rifle Association (NRA), were using gun control to frighten voters headed in our direction. I'd been picking up on this as I traveled the country. I'd get to a state, start talking to the local pols, and at a certain point they'd say, "Charlton Heston was here," and look worried.

But what I decided when the man in Saginaw spoke up was that we had to fight back. I called Nides and said, "This is really important. We can lose some battleground states unless we fight back on the gun issue." I wasn't the only person picking up on the threat; the campaign knew that it had to go on counterattack and that there wasn't much time. Its strategists turned to the unions for help. Labor quickly put together a letter and distributed it at work sites throughout the country, concentrating in particular on targeted states where they sensed guns were a problem. It said something like "We know some of you are being told by the Republicans that if Al Gore gets elected he'll take away your guns. That's wrong. If Al Gore gets elected he won't take away your guns, but if George Bush gets elected he's going to take away your right to be in a union—and maybe your job as well."

Ironically, gun control was playing out in some of the same states where Nader was cutting into our numbers, such as Oregon, Minnesota, and Wisconsin. To win these states, Gore and I needed to bring back both the Nader people *and* gun-owning Democrats—an interesting challenge. One beautiful night in Wisconsin before a rally with almost five thousand people, many of them labor union members, I told Al that I had been speaking out about our position on guns, and unless he had objections, I would do so tonight. He urged me to go right ahead. And I did: "I understand Charlton Heston was here telling you that if Al Gore gets elected he'll take people's guns away. Well, let me tell you something about Charlton Heston," I said, cribbing from the Lloyd Bentsen line, "I know something about Moses. Moses is, in a way, a friend of mine. And believe me, in this campaign, Charlton Heston is no Moses."

Then I'd say, "Let's talk about safety, and keeping guns out of the hands of criminals. That's what we want to do. Let's talk about school violence, and keeping guns out of the hands of kids, too." And I'd add some personal context.

"My home state of Connecticut has been known as the arsenal of Democracy since the Revolutionary War," I told the crowd. "We're proud to be home to the best gun manufacturers in the world: Colt, Remington, Marlin, Winchester, and Sturm and Ruger. I would not support a proposal that would deny the right of law-abiding citizens to buy and own guns."

In the end, we stopped the hijacking and carried most, but not all, of the battleground states where guns mattered. Organized labor deserves tremendous credit for the work it did on this pivotal issue, as well as so much else it did for our ticket in 2000. After the election, an analysis was done that showed we had been able to counteract the NRA's campaign against Gore wherever the labor movement was strong. But where the labor movement was weaker—as in Arkansas and Tennessee—there was no counteraction, and we lost the states. It may not be the only reason we lost the states, but it was certainly a factor.

Three days to go. Our internal polling is showing us continuing to gain on Bush. We've worked our way back from the postdebate drop, and according to Stan Greenberg, the national election is now within a couple of points. It all seemed to be coming together. Our base Democratic vote is getting fired up. Previously undecided independent voters are worried about Bush's rightist tendencies and his poor Texas record on the environment and health care, and the Nader voters are moving away from Ralph in droves. In other words, a lot of our campaigning is working.

We feel as though we are in a marathon and a second wind has just kicked in, the way it does when you're in road races and you know the finish line is near. But we also know it's still only neck and neck.

We've spent the last Sabbath of the campaign with the entire Lieberman clan—my mother, our siblings, our children, and our grandchildren—at a beautiful beachfront hotel on Miami Beach, and I'm refreshed and ready for an epic last lap around America. As my mother and father would say, "We'll have plenty of time to sleep in the next world, so in this one we might as well stay awake as long as we can to work and have a good time." That was certainly the spirit of the last three days of the 2000 campaign.

After sunset on Saturday, we begin with my much-sought-after stop in Little Havana for a cup of Cuban coffee that was strong enough to keep me awake for most of the rest of the trip. Then we're off for an airport rally in Orlando. One of my best friends in the Senate, John Breaux of Louisiana, joins us for this event. (John and I have worked so closely together in the Senate, we've been dubbed the Kosher Cajun Caucus.) John's got a suitcase with him, and he jokes that it's full of extra votes from Louisiana—in case we need them in Florida. We have a good laugh at that one after the election, during the Florida recount.

From Orlando we fly to Albuquerque, New Mexico, where we're greeted later that night by what one staff record keeper concludes is the largest motorcycle escort of the campaign. Next morning we head to Las Vegas, where I speak at two African American churches—one last chance to preach about the proper place for faith in American public life.

In Las Vegas we experience one of the few administrative screwups of our campaign. The crew of our chartered plane, the *Spirit,* announces that they've flown the maximum number of hours permitted by the Federal Aviation Administration in that time period. They're grounded—and no backup crew is available.

We're supposed to be in Oregon and Washington State later that day, both critical states. We frantically charter a tiny plane. The problem is, there are only six seats. They're filled by me, Secret Service agents, a representative of my traveling press corps, and two staff members. That's all we can take. Hadassah and the kids, most of my staff and hers, have to stay in Vegas.

◈ As I'm strolling through the Paris Las Vegas Hotel and Casino, which has an Eiffel Tower outside and a pretty incredible re-creation of the City of Lights inside, someone says to me, "It could be worse. At least we're in Paris!"

We checked into Bally's. I very much wanted to drop a couple of quarters in the slot machines downstairs, but I was terrified I'd be caught doing it. That was just what the election needed right now. I could see the headlines: MRS. LIEBERMAN CAUGHT GAMBLING IN LAS

VEGAS. Even just walking around the casino made us anxious, and Hadassah is a fairly unusual name. To avoid being recognized, we changed my name for that night. I became Linda Theresa.

We land in Oregon in the early evening for a visit to our campaign headquarters there and a media event with my friend Senator Ron Wyden, then on to Des Moines, Washington (yes, Des Moines, Washington), for a spirited rally at the university. Monday morning, I meet up with my family, staff, and campaign plane in La Crosse, Wisconsin, for a rally at the local high school; then we head to Minneapolis for a rally in the rain, to New Hampshire for a rally at the University in Durham, to Bangor, Maine, for an airport rally with former Senate majority leader George Mitchell, and then to a rally after midnight at the Warner Theater in Erie, in pivotal western Pennsylvania. I later give Al Gore a good razzing because they took him to Miami's South Beach for a grand closing rally with Stevie Wonder and Jon Bon Jovi, at the same time they sent me to Erie. "Now I understand what it's like to be VP," I told him. But the truth is, that rally in Erie was one of the most moving of the campaign. We arrived at the old theater around 12:30 at night, and it was packed—there were probably three thousand people there, a wonderfully diverse, middle-class crowd, and they were hugely emotional, all charged up because, as somebody put it, "Nobody comes to Erie like this."

"What a great rally," I said to the crowd. "It makes me want this campaign to go on for another few months!"

◈ Joseph forgot for the moment that his exhausted wife was behind him by a few steps! He looked back at me and saw the disbelief on my face. And in front of everyone in the theater, he said, "I'm only kidding, sweetheart."

◘ From Erie, the *Spirit* takes us all back to Florida. One last visit to Tampa in the pivotal I-4 corridor (Orlando, where we were Saturday night, is at the other end of it). It's here that we feel we can build a margin of victory. We check into the hotel. Hadassah and the kids go to sleep. But I have no time to sleep, so I take a shower, change my clothes, and put on my special lucky Election Day tie, which I've worn every time I've run (except one) since 1970, when I won that first primary for the state senate. And of course the one time I felt the tie had gone out of style and didn't wear it was in 1980, when I lost my campaign for Congress. So although the maroon tie with particularly large and yellowing white polka dots is even older and more out of fashion by 2000, I have no intention of being seen without it on this big Election Day. When I meet up with Al Gore at 5:30 A.M. at a Cuban American

Bakery in Tampa and explain the tie's significance, he gives me one of those wry Gore smiles. "I've been admiring it."

In the preceding twenty-four hours, Al's been doing some battleground traveling, too, from Iowa to Missouri to Michigan to the South Miami Beach rally to a hospital in Tampa for a meeting with late night health care workers at 4 A.M. So at the bakery, we are both ready for those fantastic little cups of sweet, strong Cuban coffee, *cotoritos.*

It is now Tuesday. Election Day 2000. Al raises the little plastic cup. *"L'chaim!"* he says.

"Only in America," I answer.

We fly home to New Haven to vote, a sentimental journey. Our street is decorated with campaign signs, large and small, by our neighbors, and when we go to cast our ballots at the Edgewood School around the corner, a big crowd of parents, students, friends, my Connecticut senate and campaign staffs, and longtime local political allies surrounds us. We get choked up.

We then fly south to Nashville, where we're supposed to enjoy some down time, maybe take a nap before the returns start coming in. I am known as a horse, I even think of myself as a horse, but by Tuesday afternoon I am seriously tired. The staff comes to me and says, "Senator, we hate to do this to you, but this thing is so close. . . . Could you possibly go down to headquarters and do some satellite TV and radio calls for us?" Remember, we'll have plenty of time to sleep in the next world. So I rush to headquarters.

I feel as though I'm running for the state senate again; it's that local and specific and personal. The campaign can see what a close battle this is, and we can also see, from the exit polls fed to us by friends at the networks, where we need a last, concentrated push.

I was surprised by how many TV and radio stations will put a candidate on the air during Election Day. Of course, on TV I went on mostly in small markets, and they were probably excited to finally have a chance to have a national candidate live on their station.

The exit polls in Florida are still showing the race is too close to call. So after I finish a lively call to a hip-hop radio station in Philadelphia, the staff at campaign headquarters put me on a call to a radio show in Palm Beach. It is 5:30 P.M., and the host is a woman named Randi Rhodes. She's a Democrat, and she makes no attempt to hide that from her listeners. As we start to talk she says, "You've got a very confusing ballot in Florida, have you heard?"

"I just heard as I was listening to your show, waiting to come on," I say, "and that's the first I heard about it."

"We have a serious problem," Rhodes says. "And in fact, for those who found the ballot confusing, we have an attorney at one of our big law firms" asking us to "please file an affidavit." The Democrats have already set up a phone

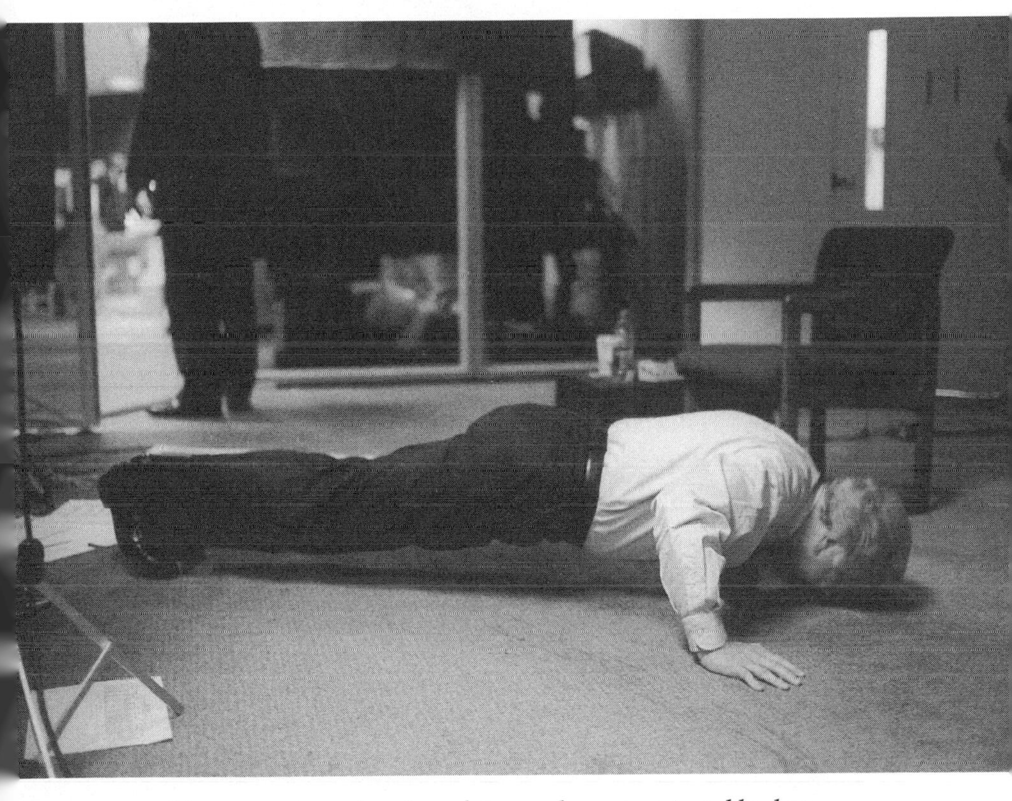

No, I am not praying. I am doing push-ups to get my blood going at campaign headquarters in Nashville on Election Day, late afternoon—before doing last-minute TV and radio interviews.

number and retained an attorney to hear voters' complaints. "I'm not sure if I voted for you and Al Gore, or Pat Buchanan and Ezola Foster," Rhodes adds.

"Wow!" I say. "Now, there's a big difference."

Randi says she must have gotten a hundred calls from people who tell her they have the same fear—they didn't vote the way they wanted.

I immediately mention these problems with the so-called butterfly ballot to the campaign staff. Gore campaign field director Mike Whouley is hearing the same story. And retired parents of campaign staffers are phoning their children in Nashville with their own takes from the Sunshine State.

But now it really is time to go back to the hotel, because the state results will soon start coming in. And I am going to try to find a few minutes to do what I've done on every election night—fine-tune the two drafts I've put together: one for my victory speech, the other for my concession speech. I cannot imagine that this night will end with my being unable to deliver either one. But as Al and I will tell each other later, "You win some, you lose some. And then there was the election of 2000."

CHAPTER THIRTEEN

It is almost 2:00 A.M. central time, and this topsy-turvy election night keeps getting more surreal. We're not plugged in; some cell phones are working, others aren't. There are four or five television sets in the room we've been ushered into, but they're closed-circuit TVs; all we can see are perplexed supporters, thousands of them, getting drenched in the cold rain outside. We're underground, in the belly of the War Memorial Plaza in Nashville, where Al Gore announced my selection exactly three months ago. This time we are here to concede the 2000 election.

What's going on? There must be a TV *somewhere* that works. In frustration, Peter Knight, Gore's chief fundraiser, pulls a set out of the wall to see if he can get it to work someplace in this bunkerlike building. Stan Greenberg manages to get through to his wife, Congresswoman Rosa DeLauro, back home in New Haven, where she's just been reelected. "What are the networks reporting?" he asks her.

It's hard to think we would believe anything the networks have to say at this point. After all, they were responsible for much of the crazy flip-flopping of the night. First, between 7:50 and 8:00 P.M., before all of Florida's polls had closed, they'd call the state for us. I was visiting a party in the hotel that my friend and relative, Pace Cooper of Memphis, was hosting for the Gore and Lieberman families, when Dan Rather announced that we had carried Florida. Everyone went wild. I hugged Pace and said, "If this holds, we'll win the election." I wasn't rushing to any early conclusions.

Two hours later, after the networks predicted Michigan and Pennsylvania had also voted for us, it seemed like we really had won and Melissa Winter and Tina Flournoy began placing thank-you calls to leading supporters. I was on one of those calls when the networks pulled Florida back and said it was too close to call. Melissa asked me what it meant, and I said, "I don't know, but it's not good." So we waited anxiously. Three hours later, with no decision in sight, I walked an exhausted Hadassah back to our room to get some sleep.

◈ I was worn to the bone. One minute we're winning. The next we are losing. It was an *unbearable* seesaw of emotions! I remember the deliberations that went into selecting "the Election Day suit" that was supposed to be so visible, and here we were, shuffling about in hotel

rooms, listening to election news reports, making phone calls into supporters' dinners bulging with people we wanted to see. The ongoing, confusing reports on states lost, states won, and others too close to call kept us frozen in the hotel, all dressed up with nowhere we could go. With embarrassment, I remember my frustration level rising to such heights that when Joe took me back to our room to get some sleep after midnight, I knocked over a huge vase of flowers in anger.

When Hadassah got into bed, she kept her makeup on in case she had to pop up and get going quickly. And that's when she and I heard the heart-stopping shocker of the night from the television in that room: "CNN is now projecting that George W. Bush will carry Florida and will be the forty-third president of the United States."

Hadassah was up and getting dressed again while I went looking for Al. We'd spent a good part of the evening with him and his family. He'd managed to stay remarkably, impressively calm the whole tense night. Now, according to one of his aides, he'd gone to change out of the jeans and well-worn green polo shirt he'd been wearing to be dressed appropriately to concede the election.

No, I thought, not yet, it's not time. My reaction was derived partially from experience with close elections and partially, I am sure, from disappointment and denial. I remember my first Senate election night in 1988, when the networks declared early in the evening that I had upset Senator Weicker but the results we were getting at our headquarters were still inconclusive. My press secretary, Marla Romash, burst into the room at about 8:55 P.M. and said, "Peter Jennings will go live with you on ABC now if you'll declare victory."

"But I'm not sure yet that I've won," I said, and I wasn't sure until well after 11:00 that night. Weicker, quite correctly, did not concede until the next afternoon. That's how close it was in Connecticut in 1988. It was even closer in Florida in 2000.

I headed toward Al's suite and on the way ran into Charles Burson, a former Tennessee attorney general who was the vice president's chief of staff and a good friend of mine. "Charles," I said. "I've been through close elections. You can't move too quickly. I think he's got to tough it out for a while, don't you?"

Charles agreed but warned we weren't going to have much luck convincing Al. Bush appeared to be ahead by fifty thousand votes in Florida, and with 97 percent of the votes in, the Voter News Service (VNS) was calculating that we would not be able to make up the margin.

Charles was right. Al's mind was made up. He felt that if the votes were not there to win Florida and thus the electoral college, then for the good of the country, he had to gracefully acknowledge defeat.

Before leading his family and advisers and my family

and team in what Carter Eskew called "a mournful motorcade" out to the War Memorial Plaza, he phoned Bush to concede.

I went to my mom's room in the hotel to wake her up to tell her myself that it was really over this time, but she was still awake, sitting there with my sisters and cousins, watching the returns on television. She had already heard the bad news. "You did a great job, Joseph, and made us all very proud. The whole family had an experience around the country we never dreamed we would have. And remember, Joseph, you only lost an election tonight. You didn't lose your life."

Hadassah had gathered the rest of the family. Becca was pulled unwillingly from her bed and hurried downstairs to the motorcade. "This was one I wouldn't have minded missing," she said later. Weeping staffers climbed onto buses. I tried to focus my mind on what I would say to our wonderful supporters in just a short while. The plan was that, in victory or defeat, I would speak briefly first and then introduce the vice president.

At the War Memorial Plaza, I try to find a quiet corner in which to polish my remarks. Meanwhile, Al's concession speech is ready and being loaded into the TelePrompTer.

People migrate from one room to another, trying to determine what to do. The word is spreading that in the motorcade coming over, Bill Daley received a frantic call from Mike Whouley coordinating the field operation in Florida. The race is tightening, said Mike, *really* tightening. VNS might not think we have much of a chance to close the gap, but Bush's margin is now down to twelve thousand—and it's falling *fast.* Daley called Gore in the lead car of the motorcade and shouted over the phone, "Whatever you do, do not go out on the stage!"

I hear all the talk, but I block it out. I have to keep working on my speech.

◈ **I point Joe out to my brother, Ary. I say, Look at him. Look at the intensity, look at his focus. I marvel at his ability to draft a speech in the midst of such uncertainty and confusion.**

Jon Sallet appears. He asks me, "Are we conceding?"

"I thought that's why we're here," I say.

▣ The door swings open. It's Al Gore. "They're telling me we're behind by less than a thousand votes in Florida."

"Then you *cannot* concede," I say emphatically.

"Damn right," Al says, "I *can't* concede." He pumps his right fist into his left hand and then into the air, spins around, and walks out the door.

The Gore family sits in chairs lined up against one wall of this cavernous room, and the campaign staff and strategists and Liebermans form a semicircle around them.

It seems absurd, but there are still no functioning televisions.

Rosa DeLauro is monitoring the networks for us in New Haven. As she's doing that, Dan Rather announces that CBS has just pulled back its declaration for Bush. Stan repeats the big news, and the room explodes in cheers just as, over the closed-circuit TVs, we see the somber, soggy crowds in the plaza suddenly go wild. They've just heard it, too.

Al says, "I've got to call Bush and withdraw my concession."

Everyone agrees, and Bill Daley says, "I'll call Evans." I'm impressed that Daley has the phone number of Don Evans, Bush's campaign chairman and longtime friend. It's a little like the hot line between Washington and Moscow. "Don, everything seems to be changing again. It's too close to call, and we're going to pull our concession back to wait for more clarity. But the vice president wants to call the governor and do it directly with him."

Daley gets the phone number for Bush. Al sits down at a desk, and I'm standing right next to him. Between our two families and top campaign staff, there must be twenty-five people in the room. It is very quiet, except for the click of a campaign photographer's camera and Al's voice, which of

The vice president withdraws his concession in a terse call with Governor Bush.

course is the only part of that historic conversation that we hear.

"Circumstances have changed dramatically since I first called you, so I'm going to withdraw my concession. . . . The state of Florida is too close to call. . . . You don't have to get snippy about it! Let me explain. . . ." Al makes it clear that if Bush winds up with a majority of the votes in the final count, he will immediately offer his "full support. . . . But I don't think we should be going out making statements with the state of Florida still in the balance. . . ." Gore stops talking as Bush says his piece, and then he interjects, "I don't care what your little brother says. The networks are all saying it's too close to call." (Al was not demeaning the governor of Florida. As is his custom, Bush had referred to Jeb as his "little brother.")

Al hangs up and says, "He didn't take it well."

It's cold, it's late. Our supporters are still out in the rain. And mixed into the crowd are hundreds of friends of mine who have flown from Connecticut and elsewhere to be with us. We had planned to join them at a big dinner our friends threw, but we'd kept waiting for the "right" time to come—and it never had.

That meant a lot of loyal supporters were still officially unwelcomed and unthanked. "Al, you and I should go out and thank our people on the plaza," I say.

"That makes sense," Al agrees.

The strategists stop us. "It's not the time to do that. The race isn't over, and it won't look right for the two of you to be out there. Bill Daley should go; you can make a statement tomorrow." (The Republicans apparently were having similar discussions and made the same decision. A large crowd of Bush supporters braved a bitterly cold and wet night in Austin and waited near the state capitol that night, but Bush never showed up. Don Evans greeted and thanked them.)

We huddle with Gore and senior advisers to draft a statement that Bill Daley will read from the soggy stage. Carter Eskew edits what many voices dictate to Gore's young speechwriter, Eli Attie. Stan Greenberg tosses in a bit of inspiration: "The battle goes on!" Then it's time for the Gores and Liebermans to disappear into the night.

"Okay, let's go!" Al calls out, and we pile back into our motorcade to the hotel. It's a very different motorcade from the one we went out on. This one is alive and full of hope.

I hadn't had more than two or three hours' sleep in the last forty-eight hours, so despite everything, Hadassah and I managed to sleep late on Wednesday, and so did the Gores.

Others were up earlier, including Hani, our twelve-year-old seventh grader who had managed to miss hardly a day of school during the campaign and wasn't going to start now. She and our dear family friend Susanne Brose flew back to Washington, and Hani got there in time to try out (successfully) for the basketball team and learn that she had been elected—yes, you guessed it, friends—vice president of her middle school. This enabled me to quip for the next few days that at least one Lieberman had been elected VP in 2000 without the need for a recount.

After a late breakfast, the Gores, Hadassah and I, and the campaign's senior people met with Warren Christopher, who had been asked to take on yet another special mission: Operation Florida Recount. When I saw Christopher, who had been so pivotal in my selection, I couldn't resist saying, "This is one hell of a mess you've gotten me into, Chris."

Al convened the meeting. We didn't spend a lot of time talking about how shocked we were to find the election result undecided on this morning after, because there was a lot of critical work to do quickly. But the fact was, we all were shocked. Even Christopher, who is famously understated, said, "This is really an extraordinary event. None of us have ever seen anything quite like it." Besides being shocked, we were also feeling proud, because we had come from so far behind and wound up with more than half a million more votes, nationwide, than Bush and Cheney. Now we had to carry the Florida recount so we could carry the electoral college and take office.

In Florida, it seemed clear, tens of thousands of voters had been disenfranchised. There had to be a way to redress that grievance. Certainly, because the results were so close, a recount was in order. In Palm Beach County, where those damn butterfly ballots had so confused voters, even Pat Buchanan, quickly and graciously, conceded that the 3,400 votes he'd received there was a preposterously large number, three times higher than his vote count in any other county. More than 19,000 ballots cast in Palm Beach County had been disqualified because confused voters had punched two holes instead of one. That's 19,000 ballots in a Democratic county in an election that was ultimately decided by about 600 votes. Other stories of improprieties were emerging from elsewhere in the state, particularly with regard to the harassment and rejection of African American voters. Our purpose in Florida after Election Day was a very American purpose: to count every vote.

Weeks later, after it was all over, I chatted with a network television reporter at a Christmas party. "You know," he said, "we were right in calling Florida for you early, because the exit polls were right: a majority of people who went to vote *did* go to vote for you."

Needless to say, that was not the Bush campaign's position. Their tactic was to portray themselves as the winners and assail us as sore losers. They released a statement saying: "The Democrats who are politicizing and distorting these routine and predictable events risk doing our democracy a disservice."

Their most unfair suggestion during the thirty-five days following the election was that "Al Gore just won't accept defeat." That was very unfair, because, as they knew, Al had accepted defeat, and with grace, on election night. He hadn't been pressed to concede (and I had advised against it), but he'd done so when it appeared that George W. Bush had won a majority of the popular vote in the state of

The day after Election Day in an elevator in Nashville on our way to the press conference at which Al said we wanted every vote in Florida to be counted.

Florida. When that lead evaporated, we concluded we would be doing our principles, our programs, our supporters, ourselves, *and* "our democracy a disservice" if we failed to do everything we could to determine what had been the will of the people in this very close election in Florida.

That's essentially what Al said, with me standing at his side, in a press conference in Nashville in front of a very large number of American flags on the afternoon of the day after Election Day.

Afterward, we flew back to Washington and everything changed. The magic carpet came to a stop. No more travel to two, three, or four states a day. No more separation from Hadassah and the kids. No more four or five hours of sleep a night and trying to catch up with naps on the plane. It all stopped.

Al and Tipper and Hadassah and I began "double-dating" again, but now to restaurants and movies instead of rallies and fund-raisers. The first film we saw had the irresistible title *Men of Honor.* (It was a great one, starring Robert De Niro and Cuba Gooding Jr.) But sometimes the days felt so unscheduled that I felt like one of the guys in the old Paddy Chayefsky movie *Marty* who'd say, "Whaddya wanna do, Marty?" And Marty would say, "I dunno, whaddya wanna do?" I could hear those lines echo when I'd call the Naval Observatory and ask, "What do you want to do today, Al?"

I was surprised by some of the things I found I missed. When a politician says he misses the press, for instance, it's a little like saying he misses a freezing shower first thing in the morning—nobody quite believes you. Well, I started missing my *nuch schleppers.* That's what my traveling press corps took to calling itself; they even had *nuch schlepper* T-shirts. At one of the early stops in Florida, at a largely Jewish condo complex, I talked about how Tipper and Hadassah had become the stars of the show. They were getting so popular, I joked, that Al and I just felt like *nuch schleppers.* Later, in response to aggressive media interrogation, I explained that *nuch schleppers* are second bananas. They are literally pulled along afterward. "Ah," said the press traveling with me, "that sounds like us." And they adopted the name.

From my earliest days in the state senate, I have tried to be accessible to the press, but it *is* surreal to *live* with the press for three months. It's strange for *them,* the creators of the fishbowl, and strange for us, the fish living in the bowl. In my 2000 campaign, both sides—both the campaign and the campaign press corps—worked very hard to develop and maintain a healthy collegiality. That's saying something these days, when the relationship between press and politician often seems like the one between hunters and their prey. And I give Kiki McLean a lot of the credit for that. She and I learned a lot from each other during 2000 about media relations.

Lydia Ramos of NBC and Yoruba Richen of ABC were on board for the full campaign. CNN came and went and used local crews. Matea Gold of the *Los Angeles Times* was there for the ride from start to finish, as were Richard

Perez-Pena of *The New York Times,* Brigitte Greenberg of the AP, Liz Halloran of the *Hartford Courant,* and Andrea Stone of *USA Today.* Reuters had pretty regular coverage. *The Washington Post* was always on board but changed its reporters every week or so. Even the old pros, like David Broder, would rotate in. But for the most part, the reporters who tended to be with me the whole time were younger.

Hani used to say the back of the plane where the *nuch schleppers* sat, separated from me and my staff by the Secret Service personnel in between, was like a bunk at summer camp and I was the activities director. And it's true: the reporters had campaign memorabilia and cartoons taped up on the walls of the plane. I'm at an age where most of them felt like my kids, so I can say now that they were good kids. They may have called themselves *nuch schleppers,* but in truth they should take a backseat to no one. They're all first-class, and rising.

What was most important now were the meetings with our legal team, coordinated by Al's former chief of staff Ron Klain and augmented by David Boies, one of America's very best litigators and a dedicated Democrat.

◈ **We had to move to a different stage. Who knew how long we would have to wait before this was resolved? On** the one hand, the election had technically ended, so the one incredibly wonderful aspect to it was that we were no longer involved in a campaign in the normal sense—no longer traveling, being away from our daughter, or being apart. But the campaign did continue. Whenever we went out to the movies, out to dinners or lunches, everyone would stand up and applaud us. Every time you'd turn around, someone would be giving you the thumbs-up. Once when this happened, Joey said to Al, "Isn't this encouraging?" and Al said, "Yes, but remember. We're still in the District of Columbia."

You could never escape the uncertainty or the tension. All we could do, day after day, was speculate about what was going on in the courts. You'd swing up, you'd swing down.

You know what was funny? The constant questions from friends and family about what was happening. We knew as much about what was happening as they knew. We were all in the same boat; we were all sharing the same information. Okay, so maybe we had an inside track from the lawyer—but what was his inside track? It was all up to the courts.

◘ While the real battles were being waged in the courts, we fought the battle of appearances and nuances. On his ranch, Governor Bush tried to wrap himself in an aura of officialdom. A few weeks after the election, with nothing settled, Bush brought in Colin Powell and started "choosing" his cabinet. We didn't. We thought Bush was overplaying his hand and that the public would react negatively to his presumptuousness.

While Bush was trying to look ready for Washington, Vice President Gore was, of course, already there, and together we also began to prepare for a transition to power publically, but more subtly. At the vice president's office in the Executive Office Building, we met with our newly appointed transition committee to discuss possible cabinet members. Then Al met with the secretary of the treasury, Larry Summers, to discuss the economy. And for the first time, Al and I talked about what role I would play in the administration.

Clinton and Gore came into office with real differences in interests and experiences. Al was especially interested in environmental protection and science and technology issues, and of course he had more foreign policy experience than Governor Clinton. It was therefore natural for Al to be deeply involved in those areas. On the other hand, Al and I had overlapping interests in foreign and defense policy, environmental protection, and economic growth.

Although I had heard talk about it, I came to understand only late in the campaign that after the 1992 election, Al had negotiated with President Clinton about what his role as VP would be, and they signed a memorandum of understanding about areas of responsibility and frequency of meetings. During Campaign 2000, a couple of my friends who had been there in 1992 had urged me:

"You've got to be ready to do the same thing. Right after the election's over, go in and negotiate an agreement with Gore." That always had seemed unnatural, and I hoped it would be unnecessary. And in the strange twilight zone after the 2000 election, it felt particularly inappropriate to be "negotiating" for anything. All the same, we had to start making plans for the future, because we needed to be ready to begin governing if the recount ended with us as winners.

One day during November, Al and I met around the dining room table at the Naval Observatory with Roy Neel, another former Gore chief of staff, who had been asked to head up our transition. Al began to discuss the relationship he'd had with President Clinton and talked about their negotiated agreement. That, he told me, is going to be the floor for the relationship that you and I are going to have. I want you to be involved in everything; we'll set up regular times to have meals and meetings together, and you're going to be right with me.

Looking back, I think one of the things that impresses me most was the degree to which we kept our spirits up over those thirty-five difficult days. The person most powerfully tested, of course, was Al Gore, and it must be said that he was remarkable. He was warm and gracious, concerned about everyone else, and his sense of humor never abandoned him. He was a real leader to us all in those weeks. And he fought well and hard for what he believed was right. He could be funny in the midst of the pressure, too. Once, he and I emerged for one of his postelection public addresses, and I assumed what Al wryly described as the "vice presidential position," which is to say, I silently stood three feet behind and slightly to the right of Gore. The next day, when various photos of the event turned up in the papers, Al studied the bunch and then singled one out. "Now here," he said, tapping it with his finger and trying to suppress a laugh, "here you are assuming *exactly* the right vice presidential expression toward me—somewhere between respect and adoration."

Shortly after Election Day, a senior person in our campaign approached me privately. "Be careful here, Joe. You're a young man. You ran a great campaign. You have a big future ahead of you. Don't come off looking as though you are prepared to do anything to win this one." I was already being seen as a hawk in the internal discussions about our legal strategy in Florida. I felt that the race was so close, there was so much on the line, that we should assert every legal right. That was my training as a lawyer. That was my experience as attorney general. And that was what both my heart and head were telling me.

"I hear you," I told my friendly counselor, "and I appreciate your concern, but I just feel we're doing the right thing here. We shouldn't be criticized for exercising our legal rights in court. And if we are, or I am, I'm prepared to take it."

On the first Saturday after Election Day, Hadassah and I

had just come back from our Georgetown synagogue, and we were eating lunch with our friends and neighbors Mindy and Shelly Weisel when Tom Nides appeared at the Weisels' door.

"The vice president wanted me to tell you that they are making some big decisions today, and he wants to know if you can come over." This was important, so I immediately said yes. "You want a lift?" asked Tom.

"No," I said. "I'm going to walk. It's not an emergency, and we can make it over to the Observatory in a half hour or so."

"Okay," said Tom, "I'll walk with you."

As we walked up Wisconsin Avenue on that Saturday afternoon, he told me that there was strong sentiment around the table at the Naval Observatory to pull the campaign out of some of the more controversial lawsuits, including one that aimed to have a new election in Palm Beach County because of the butterfly ballots, and another in Seminole County that was based on the negligent and partisan conduct of the local election officials. Tom said he agreed with the people who were arguing that we should concentrate on our request for recounts in four of the counties. If we pursued all these lawsuits, including ones that were unlikely to be successful, we would really look like sore losers. Later, Tom told me that when Gore had said he wanted me there before the decision was made, and asked Tom to go and get me, one of our campaign officials asked Tom to convince me on the way there to urge Gore to drop most of our legal claims.

I wouldn't go along. I told Tom on the walk over, and the others once I got there, that I was sure Jim Baker was not then at Governor Bush's table arguing that they forgo any of their legal claims because pursuing them might look overly aggressive to the public. The fact is, they were going to do anything they had to do to elect Bush. Then, once he was safely in the White House, they would figure out how to rehabilitate him.

I also argued that one of the things I had learned as Connecticut's attorney general was never to abandon any of your legal rights and options until you had to. "Let the courts decide how strong these claims are," I said. And that, ultimately, is what Al decided to do.

As the Florida recount battle went on, and the media coverage went round the clock, I concluded that the American people (and people around the world) were following the postelection drama more closely than they had the election. It was like a baseball game that had gone into extra innings; more and more fans kept tuning in. And as the weeks wore on, the tenor of the postelection period grew increasingly bitter as both sides vied for public favor. It was as if neither side could acknowledge that the campaign was over and the real battle was in the courts. Or maybe both sides believed public opinion might affect the courts.

For the most part, we relied on our legal team to explain to the public our view of the latest legal twists. David Boies, in particular, was excellent at this. Other times, the public relations work fell to our very credible campaign chairman Bill Daley or to me.

On Saturday, November 18, at Bush's behest, his friend Montana governor Marc Racicot came out swinging. The Democrats' lawyers, he said, have "gone to war . . . against the men and women who serve in our armed services."

Apparently, one of our lawyers in Florida, concerned about a recent flood of absentee ballots from abroad, some of which had allegedly been mailed *after* Election Day, had circulated a memo, detailing how to challenge those ballots, including ones from military personnel on foreign duty, on every possible ground. The Republicans saw this memo as a smoking gun. By the end of the day, they had put retired general Norman Schwarzkopf on television to speak out against the memo and question our patriotism.

Because Racicot and Schwarzkopf had made their statements on Saturday while I was observing the Sabbath, I hadn't seen them. I was scheduled to go on *Meet the Press* the next morning, so on Saturday night after Sabbath, I had a phone conference briefing for the show, during which the Republican attack on the Florida memo was one of several matters discussed. The next morning, Tim Russert asked if I was aware of the memo. I told him that I'd heard about it but had not yet seen it. He put up a portion of it onscreen—and I saw immediately that the language was very aggressive and inconsistent with our message in the Florida recount.

"Count every vote." That's what we had been fighting for all along. Give the voters the benefit of the doubt, the right to have their votes counted. Respect their intentions. And here was a memo that stressed disqualifying certain ballots from absentee voters on technical grounds—in other words, how to *not* count every vote. To make matters worse, the voters were servicemen and -women. I told Russert, "If I were there, I would give the benefit of the doubt to ballots coming in from military personnel generally." I urged Florida's elections officials to "go back and take another look, because, again, Al Gore and I don't want to ever be part of anything that would put an extra burden on the military personnel abroad who want to vote."

I felt strongly that I was on message. I thought I had handled it exactly the way the campaign would have wanted me to handle it. But I soon discovered that there were people in the campaign who felt I'd undercut their efforts and hurt the cause. I was prepared to fight to win as hard as anyone in the campaign, harder than many, but I believed that the memo was a mistake.

I spent a lot of time during those weeks working the phones, briefing mayors and members of the Senate, the House, contributors. A few days after that appearance on *Meet the Press,* I was on a phone conference with Dick Gephardt and House Democrats, and as we were finishing up, Charlie Stenholm spoke up. Charlie is a conservative Democrat from Texas. He said, "Joe, I just want to thank you for what you said about the military ballots in Florida because I was under tremendous pressure here. We would have been placed in an untenable position if we were seen, as a party, to be opposing the right of soldiers to vote."

Norm Sisisky, a veteran Democrat from Norfolk, Virginia, who has since passed away, chimed in. Norm had a big naval base in his district, and he said, "I was very upset when it looked as if we were trying to stop the sailors and soldiers from voting. I cannot tell you how great the reaction was after you spoke. I'm proud of you, Joe."

My television appearance nine days later was less controversial. The night of November 27, Florida's partisan secretary of state, Katherine Harris, refused to allow the recount to be completed or to include the results of the nearly completed recount in Palm Beach County, and she declared George W. Bush to be the winner of Florida's electoral votes. He had won the state, she declared, by 537 votes out of 6 million cast. The campaign asked me to respond in a live television address. From a classic room at the historic Hay-Adams Hotel, across from the White House, I denounced "what by any reasonable standard is an incomplete and inaccurate count" and declared our unwavering resolve to press forward in the courts.

Others have written at length of the legal ups and downs of that recount, so I will not try to walk you through the maze of court actions. As Bush campaign counsel Benjamin L. Ginsberg said, "This is the largest peacetime mobilization of legal talent in the country's history." But no legal action or decision was more exciting to us than the big decision of the Florida Supreme Court on Friday, December 9.

Florida's highest court ordered an immediate manual recount of thousands of ballots in three Florida counties (Broward, Dade, and Palm Beach). This was what we had wanted: a full and fair count. We had won on principle, and this, we thought, would enable us to win on the votes. But win or lose, the Florida Supreme Court decision meant a fair end to the election.

The decision came out around 4:00 P.M. I called the Naval Observatory to talk to Al, and we were both tremendously excited. He said, "You know, I may do a public statement later this evening. I know it's Friday, and it's getting late, but could you walk over here later? Everybody's excited about this and people are coming over. You ought to be here."

"Sure," I said. "I'll be there. Just have someone let me know when."

Five minutes later Al called back and said, "It just struck me: You still have time before the sunset to drive over. Why don't you and Hadassah come celebrate the Sabbath here—with us."

Hadassah and I quickly put together a movable Sabbath "feast."

◈ **So much was happening. Joe really needed to be there, and neither of us wanted to be alone; we needed** to be together. And Hani was off with her grandmother. So we packed up our Sabbath candles, our challahs, some food, wine for the prayer we say—everything—jumped in the limo with the Secret Service, and made it to the Naval Observatory before sundown.

◘ Tipper, God bless her, comes to the door and says, We're so thrilled you're here. Now what do you need to do?

◈ The place is buzzing. People are joyous, running around and watching the news on TV and drinking champagne that Carter Eskew brought over. We tell Tipper we need a place for me to light the Shabbat candles and Joe needs a place to pray. I put my Shabbat candles and challah in the dining room, and then Tipper leads us to the living room.

◘ Tipper closed the sliding doors behind us for privacy. I said my Friday night prayers, which are traditionally recited facing to the east, toward Jerusalem, so it wasn't until I finished that I turned around and realized that behind me was the Gores' beautiful Christmas tree. It was a very ecumenical Sabbath. Then we came back out and joined the festivities. Eventually most of the celebrants headed out to eat at a Washington restaurant, leaving the Gores, Donna Brazile, Philip Dufour, and Tipper's chief of staff, Audrey Haynes, to join us in celebrating the Sabbath.

◈ Quiet descended as we sat around the Gores' dining room table. Our usual routine of kiddush (prayer over the wine) and *motzi* (blessing over the bread) allowed us to share the freedom and stillness we are able to feel each Friday night as we usher in these twenty-four hours of sacred space. Tipper wisely said, "I know you don't use phones during the Sabbath, so we can put our BlackBerries away—all communication devices. Let's just get rid of them, put them in another room. If anybody needs to get us, they'll come find us."

◘ It was a memorable night. We talked about a lot of things, includi\ng the Sabbath, and all we had to be grateful for this Sabbath, and not much about politics or courts. And then it was time to start walking home.

"We'll walk with you!" Al and Tipper announced.

Oh, come on, we said. You don't have to do that. We have our Secret Service agents; we'll be fine.

No, no, they said. We'd love to take a walk, and it's a

beautiful night. So we slipped out a side exit from the Naval Observatory, and there the four of us were, around ten o'clock, briskly walking down Wisconsin Avenue. The Secret Service agents gave us some space, and the security vehicles followed at a discreet distance.

There's not a lot of foot traffic on that part of Wisconsin at that hour. The few passersby did a puzzled—or excited—double take, as if to say "No, that can't be them" or "That's them." But we kept moving, and occasionally somebody in a car going by would recognize us, beep the horn, and pump their fists in post–Florida Supreme Court victory solidarity. For the most part, we were left to delight in a great two-mile walk on a beautiful Washington night. The Gores went right up to our front gate with us. We hugged, and then they turned around and headed home.

The next morning, Hadassah and I went to synagogue, where we found much joy over the Florida Supreme Court's decision. But then, during the afternoon, Tom Nides came to our house to tell us that the U.S. Supreme Court had just decided to take the case. And we plunged from the highest moment of the postelection period to the lowest.

I had not thought that the U.S. Supreme Court would take the case. It was so out of line with their precedents and therefore both unexpected and ominous. What's more, they had stopped the recount that had been ordered by the Florida Supreme Court. So it was a total reversal of our fortunes within a day.

On Monday, David Boies was going head-to-head before the U.S. Supreme Court with the Bush campaign's lawyer, Ted Olsen. The Gores asked Hadassah and me to come to the Naval Observatory to listen to the oral arguments on television with them. Boies and his wife joined us for a postargument lunch. I had been on many phone calls with David for the past few weeks, usually siding with him and always impressed by him, but this was actually the first time I had ever met him. Boies was charming and upbeat. We discussed hopeful signs in the questioning by particular justices, but my own feeling was that once the Court took the case, we were swimming upstream.

I struggled to stay optimistic. The next day, as we intently followed television coverage and speculation from the Supreme Court, I began to take irrational hope from the fact that it was taking more than twenty-four hours for the justices to issue a decision. I managed to convince myself that maybe, somehow, they were arguing among themselves, that maybe one of the so-called swing justices, Kennedy or O'Connor, was trying to preserve what the Florida Supreme Court had done.

When the Court handed down its decision late that night, December 12, 2000, it hurt. The Bush campaign had decided correctly that the Supreme Court would enter the political fray. It overturned the Florida court's order for a manual recount of the forty-five thousand votes from the three disputed counties. I was furious.

After the decision, Al and I spoke by phone, through bitter disappointment, about the option of going back to the Florida Supreme Court. Sometime after midnight, we decided there was no point in that. The fact of the matter was that America's highest court had spoken. It was time to concede the 2000 election—for the last time.

The next evening, December 13, Hani and Hadassah and I rode to the Executive Office Building in somber silence in the Secret Service limousine. Trying to raise our spirits, I said, "This has been an incredible experience. We have so much to be grateful for and proud of. And we have so much to look forward to."

Hani's response surprised me: "Yeah, Daddy, you're going to be home a lot more." That was the pure heart and soul of a twelve-year-old daughter.

We stood with the Gore family as Al gave his concession speech from his office in the Executive Office Building. He was eloquent and healing. His remarks that night stand alongside his acceptance speech in Los Angeles as his best of the campaign. An enormous crowd of administration people and volunteers had gathered outside, and with the Gores, we walked gratefully and proudly through them to our cars. We had done all we could.

We went back to the Naval Observatory for a big party. After all we'd been through, it was what we needed and what everyone deserved. Jon Bon Jovi, who had been so devoted to our campaign, was there. I noticed him spending a lot of time on his cell phone. Apparently, he decided that the band at the party wasn't up to the occasion, so he called his friends Stevie Wonder and Tom Petty and urged them to drop by from wherever they were. They arrived sometime between midnight and 2 A.M. I'd like to be able to provide a vivid picture of Tipper whaling on the drums and Al cutting loose on the dance floor, but the truth is, I only know what I read in the newspapers. Hadassah and I left before midnight to take Hani home so she could get up for school the next day and I could get up to go into my Senate office and deliver my own concession speech from the floor of the Senate.

I had decided that was the right place to close this chapter and open the next one. To me, the Senate chamber is the people's forum. Its members represent the country. Its history is rich. Its debates have elevated those who serve and speak there. It is a place of dignity and patriotism. The speeches that have mattered most to me, the ones I'm most proud of, have been delivered from the Senate floor —my Gulf War authorization speech, a series of speeches on Bosnia, statements on clean air and climate change, and the Lewinsky speech. So it felt right to end my national campaign on the Senate floor.

But it is also true that I needed to go right back to work as a senator. I needed to do it for the continuity and reassurance that it brought me. It is my instinct, learned from my parents, not to let problems or defeats fester, but to move on. Each day is a new day full of new opportunities, so although the thrilling opportunity I had been given in 2000 had ended so disappointingly on Wednesday night, I was grateful to go back to working in the U.S. Senate on Thursday morning. Besides, I had lost an election, not my life.

CHAPTER FOURTEEN

On the morning after Al Gore conceded, Bob Dole phoned. "I'm calling to offer you membership in a very exclusive club," he said. "Only those who have lost national elections can join. Congratulations, you now qualify. And, incidentally, I'm the leader of the club, because I've lost more than anybody else."

It was classic Dole—warm, funny, self-deprecating, and very reassuring, coming as it did from someone who, after defeat, continued to be a great public servant. In the next few days, I received similarly gracious calls from three other members of my new club—Fritz Mondale, Mike Dukakis, and Jack Kemp.

Of course, I almost didn't make it into the club. We came so close to winning. People frequently ask, Do you think you won Florida? My answer is: It was as close to a tie as you can have in the votes that were counted. But I will always feel that many more people in Florida went to the polls intending to vote for us and did not have their votes counted.

A year later, a consortium of news organizations that pooled their resources and counted every vote came to the same conclusion. The reality, to quote *The New York Times,* " . . . is that Mr. Bush's victory in the most fouled-up, disputed and wrenching presidential election in American history was so breathtakingly narrow that there is no way of knowing with absolute precision who got the most votes. After all, there is no perfect way to decide which disputed ballots should be counted and rejected.

"And there never will be."

But here's what else the independent observers of the consortium concluded: If the manual recount in the three disputed counties mandated by the Florida Supreme Court, and stopped by the U.S. Supreme Court, had proceeded, Bush and Cheney probably would have won by a handful of votes. But we would have won if there had been a more thorough statewide recount that included "undervotes," ballots that the machines had originally read as indicating "no choice" for president, but which on closer examination often did reveal a choice.

Again, to quote *The New York Times,* the analysis "suggests that more Floridians intended to vote for Mr. Gore but were deterred, in some cases by ballots that were confounding even to elderly voters who are accustomed to having five bingo cards going at once."

The failure to count all the votes cast in Florida revealed a national problem that cried out for reform. After the election was over, there were reasonable estimates that between two and four million people had cast ballots throughout the country that were never counted. Our democracy should not tolerate such disparities in voting systems, practices, and technologies that stop so many voters from having their votes counted and that, particularly, undermine the votes of poor and minority citizens. Fortunately, in 2001 and 2002 several states adopted election law reforms that will make it much more likely that in future elections every vote cast will be counted. That is something good that came out of the bad way the election of 2000 ended.

When people ask me how I feel about the campaign, I often say, "I loved every minute of it . . . until the end."

That's the truth. It was an amazing adventure but the end was a very disturbing chapter in the history of the U.S. Supreme Court, so unconvincing on the merits and inconsistent with the Court's precedents, that I would be surprised if the case of *Gore* v. *Bush* is cited at all by justices in the future. This was not the way the election should have ended—with five justices of the Supreme Court stepping in to decide who won instead of letting the voters decide. It was undemocratic. Sadly, I have to agree with Justice John Paul Stevens, who wrote, in a stinging dissent, that the majority's opinion "can only lend credence to the most cynical appraisal of the work of judges throughout the land." He concluded: "Although we may never know with complete certainty the identity of the winner of this year's presidential election, the identity of the loser is perfectly clear. It is the nation's confidence in the judge as an impartial guardian of the rule of law."

At the same time, a lot went right with our campaign; and there was much to be proud of and to celebrate. Although Bush and Cheney had run a better campaign than almost anyone had expected, the fact is that Al Gore and I got half a million more votes than they did—indeed, more votes than any Democratic ticket in American history and more votes than any ticket of any party except for Ronald Reagan–George H. W. Bush in 1984. And the feared surge for Nader never materialized, especially in the states where he looked strongest and where we counter-punched hardest. Nationally, Nader failed to get the 5 percent of the votes he needed to qualify the Green Party for federal matching funds for the 2004 election. He got only 2.74 percent of the vote. But Nader did get 97,488 votes in Florida, which sure could have made the difference for us, and avoided the recount that gave the state to Bush by 537 votes. Florida wasn't the only state where Nader's vote far exceeded Bush's margin. So, ironically, it can be said that Ralph Nader helped elect George W. Bush, our forty-third president.

As for me, I eneded the campaign proud of what I had been able to contribute to it, grateful for the opportunity and exprience, and more committed than ever to advancing the New Democratic values of opportunity, responsibility, and community into the twenty-first century.

As I walked into my Senate office the morning after it was over, the phone was ringing. It was Vice President–elect Cheney on the line. I had planned to call that morning to offer the appropriate congratulations, so I started the conversation by saying, "You beat me to it, Dick," but Cheney quickly shrugged etiquette aside.

"You called me when I was in the hospital," he said, referring to a time a few weeks before when he'd suffered a mild heart attack, "and I really appreciated that. So I wanted to call you first today."

We talked about what an "extraordinary" campaign and election it had been and how our debate had proven to be a high point in the experience for each of us. I told him, "I hate to lose, but you're an honorable man, Dick, and I congratulate you and look forward to working with you." He told me he wanted to meet with me soon, but that "the principals should meet first." I agreed. Not only had this been the closest election in presidential history, but the Senate was now perfectly split fifty Democrats to fifty Republicans. "I think I'll be seeing you a lot on the Senate floor," Cheney said dryly, meaning that, as vice president, he would be called upon often to cast tie-breaking votes.

We were both aware that relations between the two parties had grown very partisan. It was clear that—if we wanted to get anything done—we were all going to have to learn to work across party lines again when the new administration was sworn in in January. I told Cheney that I was going to give a concession speech on the Senate floor that morning and I hoped that would help begin the mending process.

Bob Dole had said to me, "Joe, you've got a lot to be proud of—and you're back in the Senate. You were *so* wise to run again." I sure felt that way as I stepped onto the floor of the Senate and a wave of awe flooded back—the awe I had felt when I entered the chamber for the first time with Hadassah in 1988.

My colleague Pete Domenici (R-N.M.) was speaking, but he graciously yielded when he saw me. "This election is over," I told my colleagues. "I congratulate Governor Bush and Secretary Cheney and wish them well. . . . It is time now for all of us to come together in support of these United States and the shared values that have long sustained us. . . .

"Whether you are happy or sad with the results of the 2000 election, I do think every one of us should be grateful this morning that here in America, we work out our differences not with civil wars, but with spirited elections. We resolve our disputes not through acts of violence, but through the rule of law. And we preserve and protect our system of justice best when we accept its judgments that we disagree with most."

I said that I would be forever grateful for the depth of America's tolerance and the richness of her diversity. The fact is that my faith may have been the focus at the start of my candidacy because it was different. I was a "first." But my faith wasn't even mentioned at the end, which is just the way we wanted it to be. I wanted to be judged on my merits or demerits. The bigotry some feared never materialized. Choosing me, I told my Senate colleagues, "required personal courage and confidence in the American people [on the part of Al Gore]. Today we can look back and say that the vice president's confidence was totally justified. . . . And that is good news for all Americans—a fulfillment of the promise that America makes to its citizens that in this country, no matter who you are or where you start, you should be able to go as far as your God-given talents and individual determination will take you."

I thought about how excited Hadassah was when she had called me from Harrisburg, Pennsylvania, one day during the campaign.

◈ **This was one of my favorite moments on the campaign trail. There was a rally chaired by Jim Zogby, an Arab American friend of Joe's and mine, and organized by Marty Dunleavy, an Irish-American friend of Joe and mine from New Haven, to celebrate ethnic Americans. The turnout was enormous. There were Croatians, Czechs, Poles, Italians, Latinos, Hungarians, Ukranians—well over twenty countries and cultures in attendance, all with national flags flying. There were people at the rally who had come from countries where my family had been *murdered* during World War II. But here they were, supporting me, wanting my picture, wanting my autograph. And here I was, with my arm** around a leader of an Arab American group and his arm around me.

I wanted to cry; I *did* cry. This country is amazing! And what amazing strength immigration brings to it. Up on that stage you could feel these groups coming together, tying themselves together, bonding, in a real way, a trusting, accepting, honest way. And I'm there, wearing all my different hats—I'm the wife of the vice presidential candidate, the child of Holocaust survivors, an immigrant, a Jewish American, an American. I was so proud of my country at that moment.

And I found myself saying, "Each of us should go back to the countries our relatives came to America from and teach the people there the American lessons we have all learned about tolerance and unity and strength from diversity. That is the precious gift we have to give to the world today."

▣ Less than a year later, on September 11, 2001, we saw how true Hadassah's words were and how strong America is. Instead of weakening and dividing us, as the terrorists must have hoped, their attacks strengthened and united us in defense of our shared values and way of life. In fact, Hadassah and I feel that the freedom, tolerance, and strength from diversity that we experienced so personally in the 2000 campaign are exactly what we are now fighting to protect in the War on Terrorism.

As I told my colleagues in the Senate in my concession speech, the campaign had vindicated one of my deepest beliefs: "Anything is possible for anyone in America." I thanked them for their friendship during the preceding months, and I told them how happy I was to rejoin them and get back to dealing with the challenges and opportunities at hand. The words of faith from Psalm 30, which Donna Brazile read to me at the Naval Observatory early on the great day of the Florida Supreme Court decision, expressed the optimism I wanted to close with:

"Weeping may linger for the night, but in the morning there are shouts of joy. So, today, as some of us weep for what could have been, we look to the future with faith that on another morning joy will surely come."

As I finished, the presiding officer of the Senate for that morning, Senator Craig Thomas (R-Wyo.), said, "We are all very proud of the senator from Connecticut."

I was surprised and touched. The senator in the chair almost never makes personal comments. And Craig Thomas and I come from different political camps, so his kind words meant a lot to me, as did those of other colleagues of both parties in the days that followed.

After Al Gore decided to concede, Manny Velasquez and Mike Davis, the heads of one of my Secret Service details, came to me and said, "Senator, the policy is that, when an election is over, the detail stays with the candidate and his family for just forty-eight hours more. So that would mean that we would leave you on Friday evening. But since the VP is conceding on Wednesday night, we wondered, are you planning to go to synagogue this Saturday morning?"

I said yes, that this Saturday of all Saturdays, we definitely intended to go to synagogue. "We thought so," Manny said, "and we talked it out and thought it would be a good idea to keep you and your family company until you walked back from synagogue, so we'll stay with you an extra half day or so."

We were moved by the gesture. Through the campaign, the Secret Service had become family to us. When you are campaigning, they are right on top of you; when you are more private, they try to keep their distance. Still, they see all that you see and live through all that you live through.

When we returned from synagogue and reached our house on Saturday morning, our status had changed. We were no longer protectees, and the men and women of the Secret Service were no longer on duty. So we invited them all in for Kiddush, which is the Hebrew word for the prayer over wine but has more generally come to mean a Sabbath social hour. There were more than twenty Secret Service agents there, and since they were no longer working, I not only made the prayer over kosher wine, but brought out some beer and a wonderful bottle of Irish Mist. There were warm and emotional toasts, and a tear or two was shed. I congratulated and thanked them for successfully completing their mission. We were all still alive.

Tom McCarthy was one of the last agents to leave. He

and I bonded early when I learned he was a Providence College grad and discovered we had a mutual friend there, Brother Kevin O'Connell, whose brother Jimmy was one of my closest friends and most loyal political supporters. Tom had provided not only excellent security for Hadassah and therefore confidence for me, but reassuring counsel for us both. So much so that I took to calling him "Monsignor McCarthy." On the campaign trail, for example, when plans would suddenly shift or the juggling of political and personal commitments would make Hadassah frazzled, Tom would say something like "Remember, Hadassah, change is our friend, we must embrace change."

That was Hadassah's favorite. She repeated it throughout the campaign, with irony and laughter, like a mantra: "Change is our friend."

On that December Sabbath afternoon, as he headed out the door of our home, "Monsignor Tom" turned and said to us, "Senator, Hadassah, I have a new mantra for you. It is this: The *future* is our friend."

ACKNOWLEDGMENTS

We are deeply grateful to Al and Tipper Gore for making possible the amazing adventure we have described in this book, to the thousands of men and women who worked so hard for us in the campaign, and to the good and gifted people on our Senate staffs in Connecticut and Washington for their extraordinary public service.

We want to thank Alice Mayhew of Simon & Schuster for her vision and advice, Sarah Crichton for being such a skilled and personable collaborator, our friend and attorney Bob Barnett for his wise counsel, and Melissa Winter for helping to organize our work on this book.

Our greatest debt is to all the generations of our family, whose love and support sustained us. Baba became a grandmother to many. Bubie inspired us. Our siblings, their spouses and children, Rietta and Gary, Ellen and Bert, Ary and Judy, Adam, Jeremy, Rachel, Jesse, Sarah and Elizabeth, carried the torch for us.

Our children were phenomenal. They worked relentlessly, traveling, making phone calls, and speaking. The patience, commitment, and sage advice of Matt and April, Rebecca, Ethan and Ariela, and Hana were critical to everything we did. And our grandchildren, Tennessee and Willie, filled us with inspiration and laughter.

We want to express here a final, personal thank you to Lt. James Kevin O'Connell of the New Haven Police Department, who in his spare time and for more than three decades was, as his business card said, our "Special Assistant Plenipotentiary"—counselor, advocate, driver, representative, and friend. He died suddenly on December 2, 2001, and we miss him, his words, his laughter, and his faith. Jimmy, we heartily knew ye' and loved ye'.

Joe and Hadassah Lieberman
New Haven, Connecticut
August, 2002

Joe surprises his mother with flowers on her eighty-sixth birthday, as she speaks to seniors in Coconut Creek, Florida, November 1, 2000.

PHOTO CREDITS

Callie Shell/The White House: 232, 237

Carol Royce-Wilder: 7, 96

Harry Hamburg/New York *Daily News*: 79, 82

Jocelyn Augustino: 137

Lou Toman/South-Florida *Sun-Sentinel*: 273

Vincent J. Musi/Aurora: 109, 118, 198, 223

ABOUT THE AUTHORS

Senator Joseph I. Lieberman (D-Conn.) is in his third term in the United States Senate and was the Democratic vice presidential candidate in 2000.

Hadassah Lieberman has dedicated much of her life's work to health issues and assisting nonprofit organizations. The Liebermans live in New Haven and Washington, D.C.